Gabriel Bonvalot

Through the Heart of Asia

Vol.2

Gabriel Bonvalot

Through the Heart of Asia
Vol.2

ISBN/EAN: 9783337385224

Printed in Europe, USA, Canada, Australia, Japan

Cover: Foto ©Andreas Hilbeck / pixelio.de

More available books at **www.hansebooks.com**

Through the Heart of Asia

OVER THE PAMÏR TO INDIA.

By GABRIEL BONVALOT.

WITH 250 ILLUSTRATIONS BY
ALBERT PÉPIN.

TRANSLATED FROM THE FRENCH BY C. B. PITMAN.

IN TWO VOLUMES.
VOL. II.

LONDON: CHAPMAN AND HALL, Limited.
1889.
[ALL RIGHTS RESERVED.]

CONTENTS.

CHAPTER IX.

FROM THE AMU TO SAMARCAND.

The ruins—Patta-Kissar—Tents of the nomad and of the sedentary Turkoman—Kakaïti, training—The Kazaks—Remains of an aqueduct—Straw tent—In sight of the mountains—A quarrel—Sorcery—The court of a baffled pretender—Baïssounne—At Tchiraktchi—A justiciary—Hope ... 1

CHAPTER X.

THE PAMIR.

General Karalkoff—Project of crossing the plateau of Pamir—We start for Marguilane—No one gives us any encouragement—Choice of a pass—Precautions against cold—The encampment, lights, candles—Fire, and no delay about it—The commissariat department—Kitchen utensils—A pharmacy—The presents—Weapons—Payment in kind, etc.—Minute preparations—Apprehensions—Passes closed—How we prepare to cross the Taldik—Hope 31

CHAPTER XI.

THE PAMIR (continued).

The start for the Taldik—Saying good-bye—Going through the pass—The valley of the Taldik—Bad news from the Alaï—No more assistants—Preparing for the combat—Another world—Where are we?—In the snow—The struggle—The "White Sea"—Polar scenery—On the way to Urtak—Shepherds hemmed in by snow—The troop loses heart—A rest—Scaling the Kizil-Art—Upon "the roof of the world"—At last! ... 69

CHAPTER XII.

THE PAMIR (*continued*).

At Lake Kara-Kul—Some of the men follow, the others are sent back—We remain eight in all—A track—A find—Satti-Kul as a nurse—Numberless wild sheep—The wind—Mount Kol—Tempest in the Kizil-Djek—Abandoned—The Rang-Kul; Kirghis and Kutasses—Scenery—Negotiations—The mercury freezes—A polar night—Caprices of the temperature—Attempt to stop us—We are on Chinese territory—We do not wait for permission from Kashgar—All aid refused us—How we procure what we absolutely require 106

CHAPTER XIII.

THE PAMIR (*continued*).

Hostility of the natives—A friend of Sadik—Upon the banks of the Ak-Su, or the Oxus—News from Kunjut—The Kirghiz make off—A funereal monument—An apparition—A derelict—The debts of Satti-Kul, our guide—His flight—Refusal to assist us or sell us any provisions—Our "brother" Abdullah-Khan—The white slave—An excess of obedience—Abandoned tents—A friend—Enemies—Requisitions—The further end of the Ak-Su valley 145

CHAPTER XIV.

TOWARDS THE KUNJUT.

The outlaws—An exile—Wakhan-Darya—Langar—Wakhan types—The Kirghiz want to leave us—Diplomacy—We start for the Kunjut with Wakhis—Difficulties; provisions run short; the Wakhis make off—An unsuccessful reconnaissance—We have to return to Langar—Abdullah-Khan turns up again—We send to fetch the abandoned baggage and Menas, who was looking after them—Exacting attitude of the Kirghiz—The Chinese at our heels, but they are too late—A saint 177

CHAPTER XV.

STOPPED IN THE TCHATRAL.

We start for the Wakhan—Carthaginian traders—Sadik and Abdur-Rasul leave us—The Afghans try to detain us at Sarhad—We cross the Hindu-Kush without a guide—Meeting the Tchatralis—This time we are stopped—Our resources exhausted—The Tchatralis—Negotiations—The Anglo-Indian Government intervenes—Forty-nine days at Mastudj—We are released—Hayward—Speedy return 209

LIST OF ILLUSTRATIONS.

	PAGE
Tchochka-Guzar	2
Ghurab	3
The Amu at Termiz	4
Ruins of the Fortress of Termiz	5
Turkoman	7
Kirghiz	9
Kum-Kurghane	11
From Kum-Kurghane to Baïssounne	13
Rachmed	16
Menas and his Horse	19
Baïssounne	22
Dervish	24
Derbend	26
From Karakaval to Guzar	28
Djame	29
Cemetery of Afrosiab, at Samarcand	31
Samarcand, seen from the Fortress	33
Milkmen at Khodjend	37
Bank of the River at Marguilane	38
A Ferghana Woman	40
A Little Girl of the Country	43
Kara-Kirghiz Girl	45
Kara-Kirghiz Little Girl	47
Osch, from the Throne of Solomon	49
Makmud	50
Sadik	51
Madi	57
Gultcha	58

Abdu-Rasoul	59
Ak-Basoga	61
Satti-Kul	64
Dress for crossing the Pamir	65
Kumgane and Tchilim	67
Equipped for the Route	69
Starting for the Taldik	71
The First Encampment upon the other Side of the Taldik Pass	75
Encampment at Palpuk	79
Kara-Kirghiz	81
Crossing the Alaï	83
Encampment on the Alaï, opposite Peak Kauffmann	87
Chinese Kara-Kirghiz	90
Night Time at Urtak	93
Encampment facing the Kizil-Art	95
The Plot	97
Satti-Kul	98
Satti-Kul helping to cook	98
The Ascent of the Kizil-Art	100
Encampment facing the Kara-Kul Pass	102
Sadik cooking	104
Starting for the Kara-Kul	106
The Kara-Kul, as seen from the Pass	108
Encampment upon the Kara-Kul	111
Lagopede	115
Sadik's Capture	117
Kizil-Djek	120
In the Pass of Kizil-Djek	123
A Horse abandoned to his Fate	125
Encampment at Kamara-Tag, before reaching the Rang-Kul	127
Encampment upon the Rang-Kul, facing the Tagharma	130
Coutasses (Yaks)	131
Djuma-Bi	133
Kirghiz of the Rang-Kul	136
Pamir Horse	138
The Payment	142
Ornaments and Arkar Horns	143
Chattput	145

LIST OF ILLUSTRATIONS.

	PAGE
THE START FROM CHATTPUT	147
ENCAMPMENT UPON THE OXUS	152
AK-TACH (WHITE STONE)	154
THE TAGHARMA, SEEN FROM THE OXUS	155
MENAS AND THE KIRGHIZ CHILDREN	156
CEMETERY OF KARA-KIRGHIZ	158
KIRGHIZ WOMAN OF THE PAMIR	159
THE HANGING WALL AT AK-TACH	164
TYPES OF KIRGHIZ KHANS	165
YOUNG ARKAR KILLED NEAR AK-TACH	167
COMING UPON AN ABANDONED QUÏ...	169
CAMP OF KIZIL-KORUM	172
AT THE SOURCES OF THE OXUS	175
MENAS ON THE YAK	176
THE GLACIER OF TCHILAB	177
KARA-KIRGHIZ CHINESE (MALE AND FEMALE)	179
VALLEY OF THE WESTERN OXUS (NORTH-EAST)	182
VALLEY OF THE WESTERN OXUS (EAST)	184
LANGAR	185
THE VALLEY OF TASH-KUPRUK	188
TASH-KUPRUK	189
SADIK HAS A FALL	191
CROSSING THE BALA-GUIZINE	194
UPON THE ROAD TO THE KUNJUT	197
ENCAMPMENT BEYOND BALA-GUIZINE	201
HORNLESS YAK AND CAMEL OF THE PAMIR	203
THE PIR	206
RANSED	208
ENCAMPMENT NEAR LANGAR	209
WAKHIS	212
AT SARHAD	215
WAKHIS	217
CEMETERY AND HOUSES AT SARHAD	220
THE FIRST TCHATRALIS	222
TCHATRALI	225
MASTUDJ	227
THE METAR	229
VIEW IN THE VALLEY OF TCHATRAL	230
SIAPUCH KAFIR	231

List of Illustrations.

	PAGE
Tchatrali Woman and Warrior ...	232
Tchatrali	233
Tchatrali	234
Tchatrali	235
Tchatrali Soldier	235
Tchatrali Dancer	236
Tchatrali ...	237
Tchatrali Mollah	238
Migane at Tchatral	238
Kafir	239
Kafir	241
Man of Yaguistan ...	242
Kashmir Scribe	243
Fortress of Garkuch	244
Bungalow of Major Biddulph at Guilguit	245
Woman of Kashmir	248
Indian of Kurrachee ...	249

THROUGH THE HEART OF ASIA.

(OVER THE PAMÏR TO INDIA.)

CHAPTER IX.

FROM THE AMU TO SAMARCAND.

The ruins—Patta-Kissar—Tents of the nomad and of the sedentary Turkoman—Kakaiti, training—The Kazaks—Remains of an aqueduct—Straw tent—In sight of the mountains—A quarrel—Sorcery—The court of a baffled pretender—Baïssounne—At Tchiraktchi—A justiciary—Hope.

November 7th.

WE are at Tchochka-Guzar, where we find our baggage and horses, with Seïd, the Arab whose domestic troubles I have already described. Seïd has got fat, and is delighted to see us. We are not best pleased at having to retrace our steps just as we are reaching the goal. We can but take things as they come, and direct our steps elsewhere. There is no mistake about the pleasure which our mirza feels at being back again on the soil of Bokhara. He walks with a figure far more erect, giving his orders in short, sharp tones, while his turban is stuck jauntily upon his head, instead of being rolled in a half-hearted sort of way, and looking as woebegone as the face of its wearer. He is girt in at the waist, and puts his hand upon his sword, which he would draw from its sheath, had it not been for years stuck fast to the scabbard, which is worn out at the bottom, but not on the battle-field.

We spend the day writing letters, and looking across the river at the chain of hills at the foot of which stands Balkh, just to the north of Tchochka-Guzar. We look and look again, heaping curses on the head of the Afghans, but at the same time we try to make the best we can of the new situation in which we find our-

TCHOCHKA-GUZAR.

selves placed. The ruins of Termiz are close at hand, so we intend to inspect them carefully and make a few excavations. Allah alone knows what the future has in store for us, and it may be that the check will be but temporary. To-morrow we intend going to Patta-Kissar.

November 8th.

We pass through a country the aspect of which is the same as upon the left bank of the river. It is also inhabited by Turkomans scattered among the fields which they cultivate. They possess small patches of ground, intersected or skirted by irrigating canals, with a *sakli* (mud hut), having a flat roof, in the centre. Near the hut is a vast felt tent for the rich, while the poor have a smaller tent, or perhaps only a straw hut. With these dwellings dotted about over the landscape, now grey with autumn, the country is not a very cheerful one; while, as there is no agglomeration of houses, or anything which resembles a European village, one does not get the impression of anything like a solidly organized society. There is, in short, a want of cohesion.

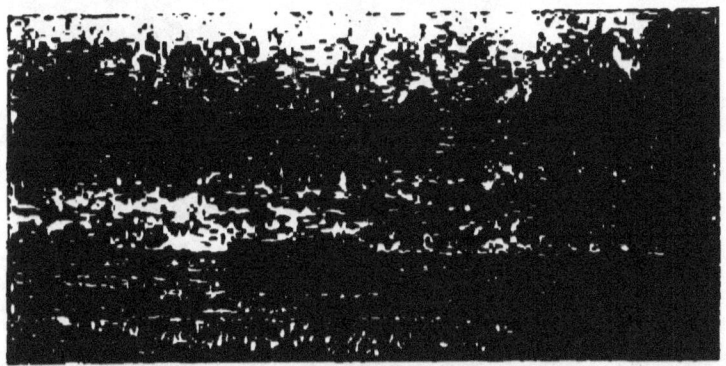

ORIBAS.

We find a lodging at Patta-Kissar, with an acquaintance of Rachmed's, a one-eyed man, with whom he exchanges vigorous embraces. He is one of the principal men in the district, being entrusted with the collection of taxes, and his fellow-citizens treat him with great respect. He formerly lived in the neighbourhood of Samarcand, but having got into trouble, he fled to Bokhara territory upon the arrival of the Russians. The father of the reigning emir received him very well and confided various posts to him; so he has at last settled down right upon the frontier, where he has become a wealthy landowner and the husband of several wives. He has also some splendid horses. He is what we should call a "very respectable" person. He has only got one bad habit, but every one overlooks that on account of his amiability.

From Patta-Kissar to the remains of the fortress of Termiz, destroyed by Gengis-Khan, is a good hour's ride. Up to the 20th of November we spent all our days among the ruins, and came back to sleep at Patta-Kissar. We worked away as long as the

THE AMU AT TERMIZ.

temperature would allow us, and so far as was possible with a few workmen provided with very indifferent tools.

I will not say more here about Termiz than that we believe it clearly demonstrable that it was abandoned for want of water; that it was inhabited by men of Turkish race who were influenced by the neighbouring populations, and whose habits differed but little from those of the inhabitants of the valley of the Zerafchane, whose history they shared. In fact, we found at Termiz very much the same objects as have recently been exhumed from the

ruins of Aphrosiab, as it is called, which are enfolded in modern Samarcand.

November 20th.

We re-ascend the valley, following the right bank of the Surkhane. At a distance of about a mile and a half we come to the commencement of the Aryk, which feeds the small oasis of Patta-Kissar. The population of this village has increased very considerably since our previous journey. The Turkomans who were the first to reclaim the reed-beds along the Amu have been reinforced by Uzbegs. The hamlet has become a small town, and a bazaar, which is very animated on market-days, has been built. A mosque will soon follow, and with a few more houses there will be a regular street.

The tents of the Uzbegs are very numerous along the river bank. They are smaller than those of the Turkomans, stronger and more pointed at the top, being regular nomad dwellings, easy to take down, to put up, and to move, the rain running off them very quickly, and the wind having little hold upon their sides. The Turkomans in this region are, as a rule, too poor to be nomad; they have not enough cattle to have any need to move from place to place, and their tents, put up between four walls, are chiefly used by them during the summer months. This is their way of going into the country.

TURKOMAN.

At a day's march we came to Djar-Kurgane. The next day we crossed the Surkhane, and in another hour and a half we reached Kakaïti.

November 21st.

The village has a fortress perched upon the edge of tall and steep cliffs, and it is inhabited by a beg. The houses below have painted thatched roofs, which is a sign of damp. The bulk of the population is composed of Torkulik Uzbegs; others call themselves Nogaï, and when one questions them as to their origin, they say—

"We come from Arka."

"Where is Arka?"

"We cannot tell you."

An old man asserts that Arka is beyond Aulie-Ata, upon the other side of the river of the Talas, not far from the land of Kuldja, where one meets people of Tsin (China).

At the foot of the Kakaïti cliffs, which form a semicircle, is a large meadow skirted by the river, with rose-bushes growing on its banks. The grass is green, amid which the cows are browsing, and there is but little blue in the cloudy sky; the scene being one which reminds one of Normandy or England. But it is suddenly animated by a troop of horsemen, who gallop up from the hollow road with shouts of joy. We see them suddenly throw a goat-skin to the ground, pick it up, gallop off, throw it down again, fight for it, jostle one another, and pursue the one who has galloped off with it. They frequently break off their game to talk, and the thing to do is to pick up the skin while at full gallop without dismounting. There is shortly to be a grand fête given by a rich man of the country to celebrate a marriage. Several goat-skins will be competed for, and the young men of Kakaïti are preparing for the jousts by training their horses and themselves.

This gathering at our feet coincides with another over our heads. A flock of rooks has assembled, no doubt in the hope that what they take for a kid will be left for them. They are resolved to have it, for they attack with warlike croaking a number of eagles which have been attracted by the same bait, the rooks being assisted by a number of magpies. The eagles are first of all driven off, and then comes the turn of some hawks, which cleave rapidly through the air, but are driven off by the magpies and rooks, which then fight among themselves. At last the rooks begin to fight each other, and they enter into the struggle with great determination. Not one of them flies away, and when they are tired with the combat they go to rest upon the cliff or upon a tree, returning with renewed vigour to the battle-field.

KAKAITI.

But the horsemen ride off, taking the goat-skin with them, thus illustrating the truth of the proverb about catching your hare before you cook him.

Beyond the Surkhane are visible the steppe and the mountains of Shirabad, and one of the natives says, "This is where the Naimans live, Uzbegs who are not up to much."

November 22nd.

We start under a cloudy sky, following the river, the banks of which are well cultivated.

As far as Min-Tout, at the extremity of the large and small aryks, we see large or small villages, which are like fruit hanging at the extremity of the branches and sprigs which diverge from the trunk of the Surkhane.

Before reaching Min-Tout, where we cross to the right bank, we notice some two-humped camels, which we had not seen for a long time. Their presence in this country of dromedaries surprises us not a little, for they make us feel as if we had left the warm countries. They are smaller than the dromedaries, with longer hair and smaller heads. But they have two humps, two "silos" in which they store a double reserve of fat in order to be able to resist the severe winters and endless snow-storms (*bouranes*).

"To whom do they belong?"

"To the Kazaks" (Khirgiz).

"Where do these Kazaks live?"

"In the Kulab. Wherever you see white camels, you may be sure they belong to Kazaks."

The Kulab is a mountainous region to the east, near Pamir; it is very cold there, for the altitude is very great, and only northern animals can live there. In mountainous countries, one finds northern climates as one ascends; altitude is latitude converted into height.

At Min-Tout (the thousand mulberry-trees, probably so named because mulberry-trees formerly abounded there), we cross the Surkhane, with its steep cliffs full of crevices, and we are again in the barren steppe, in a regular Central Asian country. One might fancy one's self near the Ablatum or the Tedjene, in the neighbourhood of Sarakhs.

Rose-bushes wave about in the bed of the stream, which eddies around them. They fill up the ancient beds, some of which are a mile and a quarter broad.

Then we come upon the ruins of the tomb of a saint, near a mound on which are fragments of the wall of an ancient fort. In the river are visible the remains of a dyke, over which the garrison of the fortress doubtless had to keep watch.

Near the river, in a bay of the bank, we see Tachtugai, and then at Kich-Kupruk, about four miles and a half before reaching Kum-Kurghane, the remains of an aqueduct going southward, about

KUM-KURGHANE.

eighty paces long, so constructed as to intersect a torrent coming from the west, and used, as we are told, to serve as a conduit for the water taken from the Surkhane, further up stream, near Dinau.

Beside the aqueduct made of burnt bricks, are the ruins of houses built of the same kind of bricks. These are traces of the grand canal which brought water to Termiz, and which had formerly made a great city of it. The artery was severed, and it dried up, life fading out of the body which it animated. In the absence of water, the city could not exist. It died of hydroragia, to use a medical term, and it is not the only city in Asia which has had the same fate.

In these latter days, the administration of Bokhara has shown a certain amount of activity in utilizing the water of the Surkhane, fresh aryks having been cut and villages having formed very rapidly.

We halt at Kum-Kurghane, where we take shelter from the rain under a reed hut, or rather under a tent which is round in shape like one. At about a level with the head, hurdles have been erected, and resting on them are four stout hoops connected by horizontal hoops, which are themselves bound together by smaller hoops, like the iron frame of the roof of the Paris Corn Market. This is the framework that bears up the roof, which has a hole pierced through it. Inside, the leaves of the reeds hang down like so much hair, while outside they are tied together with creepers, so as to resist the fierce gusts of wind. By way of pegs, we have the stems of the bamboos, which are intertwined into the hurdles, our dwelling having the style and shape of the Pantheon at Rome, but with more elegance.

We do not have at all a bad night on the matting, near the fire which has been lighted in the hole dug in the centre of the floor.

November 23rd.

We must have four horses this morning. They were asked for yesterday from the chief of the village, who was told that we would pay whatever was necessary for them, and he promised that everything should be ready at daybreak. I could not hear them being loaded, and the *aksakal* (white beard), raising the curtain of the doorway, said, with an air of consternation—

"The Uzbegs are a savage people, and they will not obey. They say that the route you have to travel to-day is a bad one, and none of them will give you any horses."

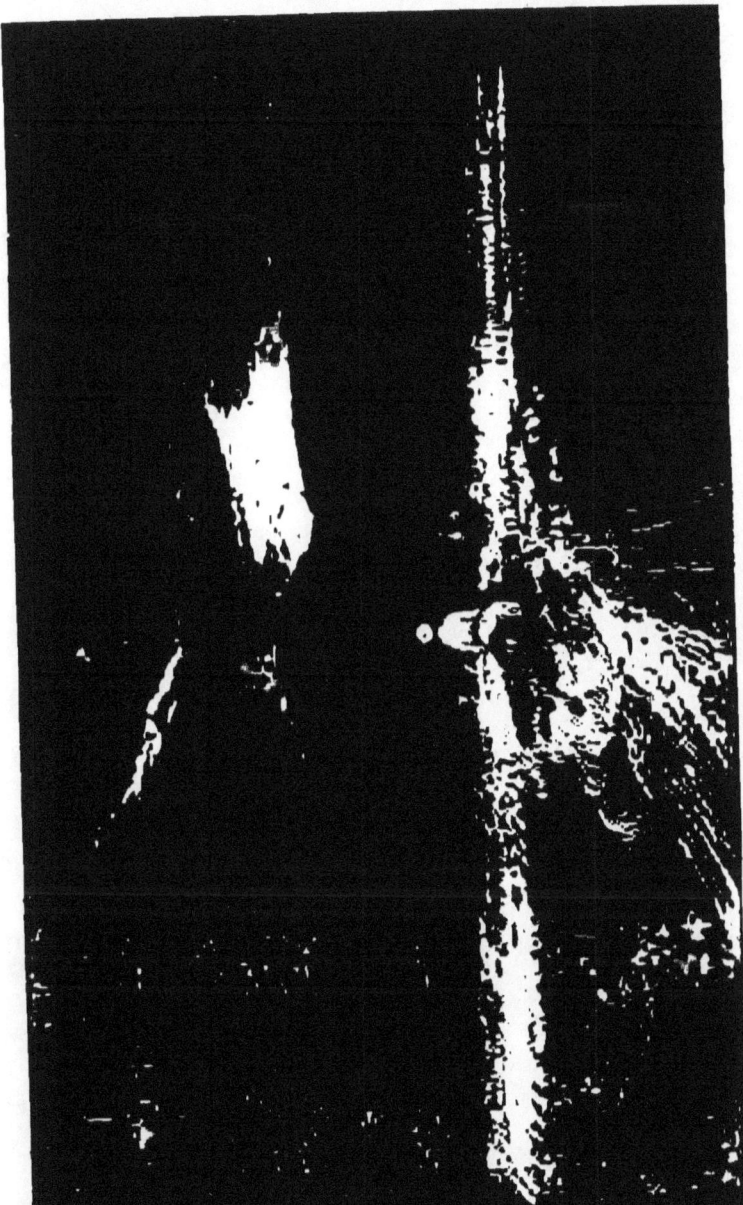

FROM KUM-KURGHANE TO BAÏSOUNNE.

I tell this to Rachmed, who is getting the tea ready, and he says—

"Do not be alarmed. Before you have drunk your tea, we shall have the horses."

He goes out, and I hear a lot of loud talking, followed by a howl, and Rachmed returns.

"What have you been doing?"

"I have beaten the aksakal."

"Why?"

"To get the horses."

"Are you sure of this?"

"Vallah! You will see the horses arrive in a very short time. Moreover, my father has often told me the same thing, and I have repeated it to you. If you are kind to the people of this country, and if they are not afraid of you, they will at once think that you are a donkey, and they will try and find a pack-saddle to fit your back. But beat them, and they will cringe to you at once. My father told me this, and I have had a score of opportunities for proving that he was right."

The horses are brought up and loaded, and we march away from the Surkhane in a westerly direction towards the mountains. The mist clears off, and we can see that we are in the plain, that the road leads to a sort of *cul-de-sac*, the two sides of which are represented by two parallel spurs of the chain which rears its wall opposite to us, and the flanks of which are festooned in the filmy clouds. Higher up, in the far distance, we can distinguish long lines of snow near the summit.

We trot forward upon the level, along a path which winds among the fallows, where the grey partridges are searching for food. We come upon the bed, nearly filled up, of a canal running from north to south, and the steppe begins again. Our attention is attracted to some large birds, with enormously long necks and unsteady gait; they are a flock of black swans which have just alighted, tired out by a long flight, and half famished. They are on the look-out for their morning meal, which will be a meagre one, I warrant.

Then we pass between some bare hills, but in the ravines below there are a great many flocks. In three hours' time we reach the further end of the *cul-de-sac*, and we begin to climb. Having made the circuit of several hills, we find, in a small valley, wells, cattle, and tents—a winter encampment of Uzbeg Kungrads.

RACHMED.

The water is salt, and we have brought to us in the mosque some koumiss made of camel's milk. It is not equal to mare's milk.

We continue our journey, and two of the horses fall lame, being all of a sweat and trembling from head to foot. Rachmed goes to an aoul situated in the bottom, to the right of the path, with the intention of hiring some horses and confiding the others to the Uzbegs, who will bring them on to us by slow stages to Baïssounne.

We wait with Pepin, who has had to borrow Rachmed's horse.

All of a sudden, I see a number of arms raised in the air, a medley of people, and hear dogs barking. There must be a quarrel of some kind going on, so I gallop to the spot, where I find Rachmed, with his turban knocked off, and his garments in disorder, surrounded by men armed with cudgels, while a tall fellow comes out of his tent sword in hand.

In answer to my inquiry as to what is the matter, Rachmed says that they have been beating him. But if he has received blows, he has given some as well, for several of the men let me see that they are bleeding. All around me are men howling, cursing, and threatening. All of a sudden, Menas makes for these men, but Caucasus fashion, with his kindjal in his hand. This unexpected reinforcement puts them to flight, some making for the mountain and others for their tents, one of them being slightly wounded in the back. I have the greatest difficulty in keeping back Menas, who had not seen the whole affair, and who thought that we were in danger. I calm down the two devoted fellows, and then the women folk and the old men intervene. A grandfather, who leans upon a staff, bent double, remonstrates with the men of his tribe, reproaches them with having transgressed the laws of hospitality, and orders them to provide two horses. He endeavours to palliate the conduct of these "lunatics," as he calls them, and he gives us his word that our horses shall be brought back to Baïssounne. I make him a present, and everything calms down.

Rachmed rolls up his turban, Menas puts back his knife, and we pursue our journey along the bank of the stream of salt water. I reproach Menas with using his knife without my permission, and his explanation is—

"From the distance, I could not see very well. I thought they had attacked you, and I hurried to your assistance. You know the custom, that when one has drawn his knife, it is a disgrace to sheath it without having used it. I thought that they had struck you."

The valley was dotted here and there with fragments of rock, which had fallen from the heights above; and these landslips were of recent occurrence, for we heard several fragments fall with a loud crash as we went along. The bed of the river will in time be choked with them, and it seems as if some hidden force was bent upon levelling this corner of the earth.

that some genius of the mountains had sworn to grind the stone to powder.

In a few more centuries the colossal strata of grey chalk which alternate with white marble, and which Pepin compares to slices of ham, will have crumbled away. They will no longer threaten the passer-by with their alarming crevices, and the immense grey slabs flecked with green lichen will become the very fine sand of the brackish stream upon which they now frown down. Where the strata end, the slabs are in a slanting direction, and seem to prop up the mountain itself.

We make north-north-west. Right and left of us are gorges through which trickle tiny streams of salt water. More than one of them is already dried up, leaving as the sole vestiges of its passage and as the proof of its ephemeral existence a few small pools in the hollow parts of its bed. Numberless grey partridges come to drink at them, and these birds are excellent to eat.

The paths are very steep. At nightfall, Menas and I, who form the rear-guard, find Seid driving Menas's horse before him. This is a Turkoman colt, to which his owner is greatly attached, and which he calls by the Russian name of Maltchik (little boy). Seid explains that the horse cannot move, and we find, in effect, that this is the case, and that he is bathed in sweat, with his tail drooping, his ears down, and his eye very dim. Just as we are preparing to go forward, Maltchik falls, his limbs stiffen, and he breathes heavily. Menas is in despair, and exclaims, " He is going to die; I know he is. It is better that I should die myself!"

I do my best to console him, and say, "Your horse is not so bad as you think. He is young, and will recover. And if he dies, I will buy you another. He is but a horse after all."

At the bottom of the path, a few hundred yards below, we

can see the fires of an aoul, with figures passing before the flames in the open air. We can hear the hum of voices and the barking of the dogs, which have no doubt smelt us. Seïd hails the grey beard in the name of the Tura of Baïssounne, upon whose territory we are. The aksakal arrives with three of his men, wielding large cudgels, which are the favourite weapons of these people.

MENAS AND HIS HORSE.

Seïd introduces us, and Menas relates his story and lights a candle, which he places in one of those Venetian lanterns which he never has out of his possession. The old man looks at him and shakes his head. Menas follows his gestures with anxiety, and asks his advice. He says, "The horse is very bad, but my ancestors have transmitted to me the means of curing him; I am about to recite a prayer."

He removes the cloth from the horse, which has been set on his legs, pulls his tail, pinches his nostrils, and then, removing his turban while he murmurs a prayer, which Menas mumbles after him, he rubs the back and quarters of the sick animal; and when, finally, the Mussulman puts his hand up to his beard and exclaims, "Allah, Akbar" (Allah is great), the Christian follows his example. For Menas, though an Armenian and a Christian, has been brought up in the East among Mahometans, and he has the same habits and ways of thoughts, and, if he has not their beliefs, he has a good share of their superstitions.

Maltchik is whipped to make him move, but he will not budge an inch. He is soaped over with water brought from the aoul, but this does not produce the least effect. He again sinks on to his side and begins to blow. With his long beard, his ascetic spare frame, his sheepskin, and his greasy cap, the old man, as seen by the light of the lantern, looks quite like a sorcerer. He must inspire Menas with the utmost confidence, for when he abruptly says—

"How much would you give to see your horse cured?"

Menas replies, "Whatever you like."

He then asks for five *soum* (roubles).

I do my best to stop this piece of foolery, and urge Menas not to listen to the nonsense of this haphazard enchanter. But it is all to no purpose. He unloosens his purse and begs me to let him pay the money. So he hands over the five roubles to the old man, who says—

"You must strip yourself quite naked, take your horse by the tail, kick him three times on the quarters, and I, during that time, will recite a prayer taught me by my grandfather, and which I am the only Kungrad who knows."

I point out that we are in November, that all this so-called sorcery is idiotic, that his horse will not be cured by it, and that Menas runs a risk of getting inflammation of the lungs. But the obstinate fellow will not listen to me.

"I would rather die than my horse. I beseech of you to move away. Let me do as he tells me."

"Why are you so obstinate? Why not believe me?"

"When all hope seems gone, and when one has already listened to the advice of intelligent people, it is well to listen to the advice of a silly person, if only for once."

Thereupon he begins to cry; so I can only leave him to himself. I ask for an Uzbeg who will show me the way, for the night is very dark; and I leave the poor wretch to the tender mercies of the magician. After having crossed several streams and canals, which indicate that the valley must be rather a wide one; and having met several kichlahs, whose dogs bark at us, I arrive, half-frozen, at Dachtighaz (the plain of geese). We pass the night in a tent.

Menas came in at four a.m. His horse is better, and he relates to me with much amusement that he undressed, but not to the skin, as the old man was pleased to let him keep on his leather breeches (*tchalvar*).

Upon November 24th, we arrive by the hills at Baïssounne, which extends from north to south, picturesquely situated upon a plateau and upon the gentle slopes of the mountain, which to the left of the road is very steep.

November 25th.

We receive a visit from the chief of the tura's police, a very handsome man, richly attired, with a steel axe in his belt, who asks, with no end of bowing and scraping, after our health, and inquires at what hour we desire to see the man who was so near being Emir of Bokhara. Such is the custom, and we conform to it. The kourbache advises us to select one p.m.; and at that hour he comes and fetches us, in order to introduce us. He goes on in front, with a long staff in his hand. We have left our horses at the entrance to the fortress, just in front of the guard-room, in accordance with etiquette, which appears to be very strictly observed.

The palace has not the imposing appearance of that at Hissar, nor is there anything picturesque about it, being a congeries of mean-looking buildings surrounded by a dilapidated wall.

Under the first portico are drawn up a number of men very brilliantly dressed and with very long faces. One of them speaks in an undertone to the kourbache, who asks us to wait. None of

BAÏSSOUNNE.

the people here seem to have very cheerful looks. Our introducer, who has disappeared down a passage, comes back, and he appears to be uneasy and much upset. Can it be that his master is in a bad humour?

We go down a long passage. A door to the right leads into a large courtyard, it appears, and then there is a fresh halt. We are asked to wait a few minutes, and I look at Rachmed, as much as to say, "What does this mean?"

He said that he expected the chief of police did not like to let us into the grand courtyard until he was sure that the tura was ready to receive us.

The man with the staff came back soon after, and said, "Pass along," bowing almost to the ground. We enter the room, where the master of the palace, very simply dressed, was standing up with a few of his followers about him. He shook hands with us, pointed to some stools and sat down, we following his example.

Rachmed acted as interpreter, and we first asked after his health. His answers were short, and he merely said that he was very well. I endeavoured to draw him out, explaining to him the object of our voyage, whence we have come, where we wish to go, and so forth. But he merely bows his head, without opening his lips.

While Rachmed is translating what I have said into more flowery phrases, I have a good look at him. He is tall and rather inclined to *embonpoint;* his beard, which is very black, is not thick; he has a hooked nose, the eyes large, compared to those of the Kirghiz, elevated at the corners, and very black, very brilliant, and full of motion. His head had little character about it, being that of an Uzbeg, with prominent cheek bones, and rather clumsy.

What a lugubrious-looking individual! He is yellow and bloodless. His hand is devoid of character, short, thick, regular in shape, and white—the hand of a strong race which had for generations done no work. But for his eyes he might pass for a wax figure.

He had the anxious look of a man apprehensive of misfortune, and the sad look of one who has just lost a dear friend. He is mourning for the loss of a throne, and his regrets are easy to understand. We take leave of him after a few minutes' conversation, or rather monologue. He asks us, however, one question as we are leaving, and that is, how long it is since we left our country, but this is all. We again shake the hand which was so near wielding the sceptre and withdraw.

DERVISH.

The kourbache, who is waiting for us at the door, says that he has been instructed by his master to tell us that " Baïssounne does not belong to him, but to the Russians, and that we may do as we please there." As soon as we are alone, Rachmed puts his hand up to his face, which is equivalent to saying that he can with difficulty restrain himself from laughing. After he has had his laugh, he sobers down, and, referring to the painful situation of the tura, he says—

"One can understand his not being very cheerful. Do you notice that he looked like an ox which has been driven out of a fat pasture by another ox. He has taken refuge in the midst of an aoul, and he is surrounded by men with cudgels, ready to strike, while his eyes are nearly starting out of his head."

The bazaar at Baïssounne is full of animation, being the rendezvous of the Uzbegs, who come there to dispose of their barley and stock. We see no sign of any Russian goods, and the shops are of anything but a luxurious kind, the gallows alone being in good order.

In the courtyards of the houses stand a number of tents made of felt. For Baïssounne, which, with its five or six thousand inhabitants, might be taken for a town, is no more than a very large kichlak, the inhabitants of which have preserved the customs of the aoul. At each step one meets cows and donkeys; there is an abundance of stock in the fields, trusses of hay upon the roofs, huts, and vine-clad gardens. Upon the large square, beyond the ravine-like river of Basrikun, with its narrow and pebbly bed, a number of horsemen are amusing themselves with the goat-skin, as described above, while the women look on from the roofs above, with their hands over their eyes, bent forward, and clad in long, dark dresses. The stock is allowed to browse in the cemetery, and the place is a regular winter encampment.

From Baïssounne we proceed to Derbend by a picturesque and very wild road through a mountainous desert. Derbend is pleasantly situated in a bottom, upon the banks of a stream, at the meeting of several valleys. It is a very peaceful corner of the world, and would suit a Trappist. The inhabitants of three or four scattered hamlets, including about fifty tents, claim to be Tchagataï, and they speak Tadjik. An Uzbeg contemptuously describes them to us as " Ietiuruk ; " and the nickname of those whose genealogy is very mixed is " the people of seven kinds." In Central Asia, the people of Turkish blood despise those who have " lost their race."

From Derbend, going back to north-north-west, and then

DERBEND.

taking a north-west course, we arrive, by the celebrated pass of the Tchaktchak, first at Karakaval, which is at the bottom of a regular well, and then at Kalta Minor. This mountainous region is very desolate and lonely, the only signs of life being a few kichlaks of Uzbeg Kungrads in the recesses of the valleys.

From Kalta Minor we go to Guzar, which we had already visited during our previous journey, and thence to Tchiraktchi by Karabag.

Wherever we stop, we are questioned about the railway, and are told about the war which is about to break out, there being a general feeling of uneasiness. At Tchiraktchi we notice the absence from the fortress of the turadjane, the brother of the emir, who used to reside there, and we are told that he has gone clean out of his mind, and that it has been necessary to take him to Bokhara, where his brother has had him put into close confinement.

Others say that he had taken the part of the Tura of Hissar, for he was surrounded by a number of ambitious and discontented men, who exercised a very pernicious influence upon him. It was in order to reduce him to reason that he was lured to Bokhara by specious promises, and to repair the mischief done by this weak-minded ruler, the emir had sent to Tchiraktchi the energetic beg who receives us.

He is a tall and very taciturn old man, with a white beard, arrayed in a rich fur robe from Karakaval, and constantly moving about in his residence. He has the reputation of being very rich and very near. He keeps a close supervision over the workmen employed in repairing the fortress, which was in a very dilapidated condition. He is having the walls rebuilt, and closing up all the issues to the river Aksu, whose shallow waters flow at the foot of the cliff, and form one or two islets in midstream. There is a fine view from the windows, but this does not interest the beg, who cares little for the sight of the rice-fields, the tents in the steppe, the white summit of the Hazret-Sultan, the giant of the mountain chain on which the Uzbegs graze their mares. He takes no heed of the majestic herons by the foot, the lowing of the oxen as they are led to drink, or of the camels with their tinkling bells, who grunt angrily because they are not allowed to drink as they cross the ferry; but he likes to question travellers, and to examine the goods of passing traders. He is not averse to having a specimen offered him, and he is very hard upon all about him.

His master has sent him here to put the finances and the administration in order, and has bidden him punish severely the slightest attempt at rebellion. Without losing any time, the beg had the most guilty cast into prison, and it is said that he had a few of them executed. We can see through a half-open door four personages of importance crouched down in a corner, under

FROM KARAKAYAL TO GUZAR.

the strict guardianship of four men armed with lances. They are dignitaries, amlakdars, mirakhors, etc., accused of jobbery.

During the day, the prisoners' feet are chained together, but at night-time one of their legs is tied to a beam. Their food is supplied them by their families. Rachmed had seen one of them at Samarcand, and put some questions to him, which the latter does not dare to answer before the warders.

The prisoner expects that they will all be put to death; but he, like his companions, is resigned to his fate. But they will not be executed publicly; they will be taken to Bokhara, and there they will be made away with, their death being kept secret.

We ask the relentless beg who they are. His reply is—

"They are bad men, and there were many more of them when I came into the country, but they fled and took refuge

DJAME.

upon the territory of the Russians, who ought to have had them arrested and handed over to us."

"What would you have done with them?"

"We should have punished them as they deserve; and they would have been a great example to others."

From Tchiraktchi we went to Djame by the undulating steppe, along the slopes of the Samarcand-Tau mountains, and the next day we were at Samarcand. We returned with a feeling of annoyance at our failure, but not altogether disheartened; and we said to ourselves that perhaps circumstances would favour us another time. In short, we preserved a vague and ill-defined hope, but still sufficient to induce us not to lose patience, and to watch for the first opportunity.

CEMETERY OF AFROSIAB, AT SAMARCAND.

CHAPTER X.

THE PAMIR.

General Karalkoff—Project of crossing the plateau of Pamir—We start for Marguilane—No one gives us any encouragement—Choice of a pass—Precautions against cold—The encampment, lights, candles—Fire, and no delay about it—The commissariat department—Kitchen utensils—A pharmacy—The presents—Weapons—Payment in kind, etc.—Minute preparations—Apprehensions—Passes closed—How we prepare to cross the Taldik—Hope.

DECEMBER, and here we are back in Samarcand. We put our collections in order, pack them up, and write as many letters as we can. We are by no means satisfied, and are undecided as to what we shall do. My readers know that one does not readily abandon a project which one has caressed for years. Checks, in a case of this kind, accentuate the desire to succeed rather than kill it, and, even when in a sinking boat upon an angry sea, one does not lose hope, saying to one's self that the wind will perhaps drop, the sky clear, and a gentle breeze take one safe into port.

So we have one eye fixed upon France and the other upon India, and we are bewailing our luck, when we learn of the arrival of General Karalkoff, who has shown so many proofs of sympathy with France, and who, during our previous journey, gave us so many proofs of friendship and so much assistance. This piece of news is like a ray of light in a dark sky, and we say to ourselves that something will assuredly happen. General Karalkoff is one of those who know Central Asia better than any one; he is a general, an administrator, and a man of very large ideas, such as France so urgently needs. His arrival is sure to make a modification in our plans; and he will tell us what he thinks of the other roads leading to India.

After a long conversation with him about the Pamir, Kashgaria, and the recent journeys undertaken in this region, the general says to us—

"Why should you not try to enter India by Kashgaria, or even by the Pamir? No attempt has ever been made to explore it in winter, and the enterprise is regarded as hopeless. But who can tell? It might be worth trying."

These words were like the breeze so anxiously desired by the mariner, like the puff of wind which causes the fire smouldering beneath the ashes to burst out again. So we go back to our maps, cross-question the hunters and the natives, read the travels of Forsyth, Putiata, Ivanoff, Regel, etc., and speedily decide to go to Marguilane, where we shall be better able to collect information, prepare for our journey with the assistance of General Karalkoff, who offers us his hospitality, and start, if it should be decided, either for Kashgaria or the Pamir. We have no doubt as to the first route, for the information of the caravan men is

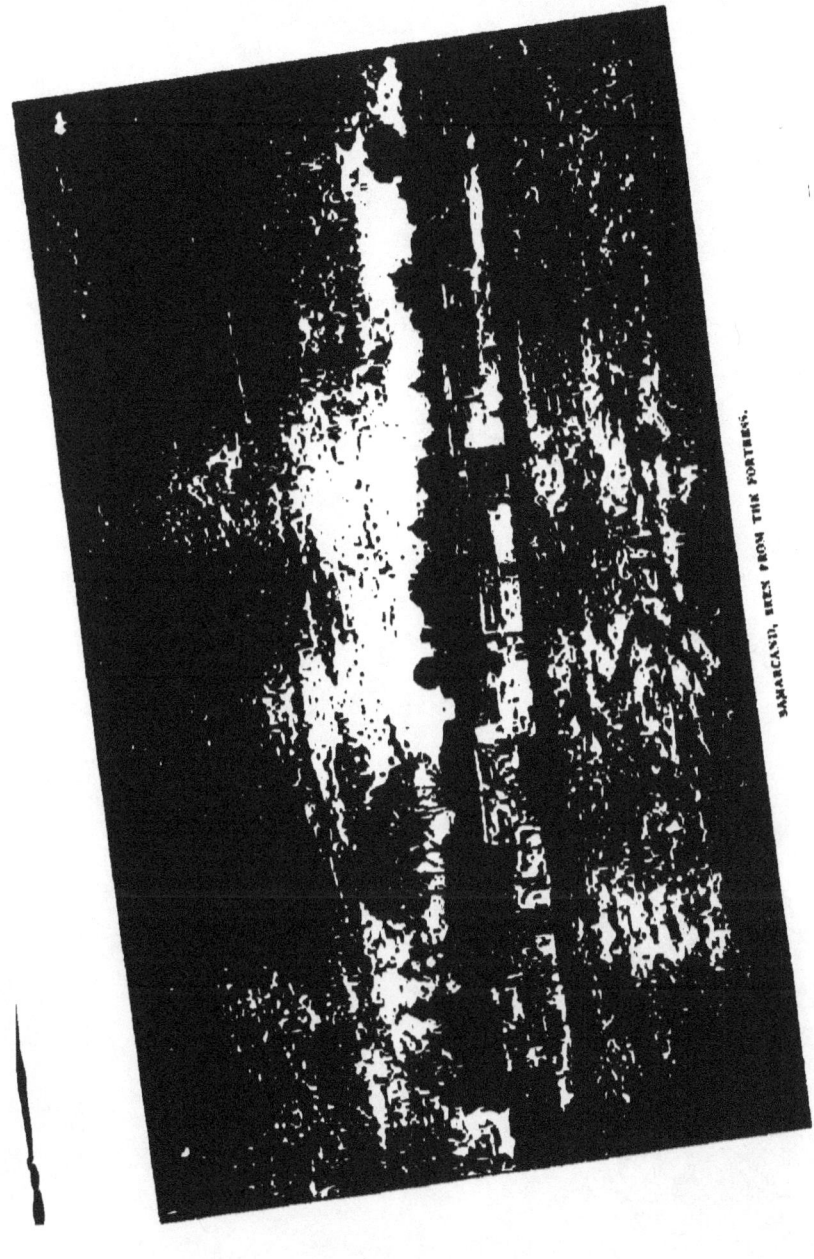

SAMARCAND, SEEN FROM THE FORTRESS.

positive that it can be taken in winter, going to Ladak by the Terek-Davan, Kashgar, Yarkand, Kargalik and the passes of Karakurum. This will be a *pis-aller* in case the Pamir should be totally impracticable, for we have but very vague information as to what winter is like upon "the roof of the world."

When we speak of our intention of passing over it in February or March, people smile, and our acquaintances look at us with amazement, give us to understand that we are mad, and urge us to give up this project. In fact, no one thinks we are serious when we speak of the Pamir. We are not very decided upon the point, and make no attempt to confute the objections raised, waiting until we get to Marguilane.

We send Rachmed and a few men on in advance with our baggage and horses, and as the road is bad, they will take about twenty-five days to reach Marguilane. Having settled our affairs, we say good-bye to our friends, and upon the 14th of January, our old acquaintance Barchefski accompanies us as far as the Zerafchane. After a parting hug, we cross the "gold-rolling stream," which has less water now than in summer, and we make for Djizak in a sleigh, travelling by way of Zaamin, Ura-Tepe, etc., by the seven cities which Alexander captured. At last we reach Khodjend, built upon the Sir-Darya, which the famous conqueror no doubt crossed at about the spot where the Russians have built a bridge. Upon this occasion, we merely walk along the banks of the river, and start for Kastakos on wheels.

Kastakos is in the midst of an arid steppe, exposed to easterly winds which blow nearly all the year round, while the Sir-Darya drifts ice almost ceaselessly. Still, even this motion gives a little life to the motionless plain. We again see Khokand, with its vast bazaar and countless victims of goitre.

Early one morning, we come within sight of the barracks of Russian Marguilane, then of the church in the principal square, and we go to stay with General Karalkoff, whom we find suffering from indisposition, but kindly disposed as usual.

The Governor of Ferghana, who inhabits Marguilane, the capital of the province, is also an old acquaintance, and he is very ready to do what he can for us. We thank him very heartily for this. At Marguilane, we are not quite at the foot of the wall, but we are not very far off.

In clear weather, we can easily distinguish the chain of the Alaï, from its lowest spurs to its summits. At times the highest peaks disappear, and then we feel uneasy, for we know that snow is falling. When the mist clears off the horizon, the mountains stand out whiter than they did before. We are always going outside the town to "see how they are getting on." If the passes of the Alaï were impassable, we should have to give up our project of crossing the Pamir. For I ought to have said that, after collecting all the information we can get, we have resolved to make the attempt. We have discovered two persons who think we are sure to succeed, General Karalkoff and Captain Grombtchefski, a very hardy young officer who has travelled in the north of the Pamir during the summer. According to him and to the Kirghiz chiefs whom we have questioned, there is very little snow on the plateau of the Alaï, which precedes that of the Pamir ; the pass of Kizil-Art, situated beyond that plateau, is still open, and we should have little difficulty in reaching the " roof of the world." Once upon this roof, there would not be much difficulty, the snow not lying to any depth. Beyond that point, they are not able to say much, but they think we might go straight to the Kanjut, and so reach India. According to the Kirhgiz khans, the difficulties would be at the beginning of the journey, not at the end. The main part, they say, is to get through the passes of the Alaï, and carry enough provisions to last a month.

According to the persons who are opposed to our making the

journey, and who reason after their own experience of the Pamir, or what they have been told, not only shall we be unable to cross the Alaï, but we shall be buried beneath avalanches of snow. As to the plateau of the Alaï, it is unquestionably a mass of snow, and so, too, is the Pamir. According to the great majority of the pessimists, we are marching to certain death. But upon one point every one is agreed, and that is that the Pamir is almost entirely uninhabited, and that we are certain not to encounter many of the plundering Kara-Kirghiz, who would arrest our march in the

MILKMEN AT KHUDJEND.

summer. If the region is not free of snow, it will be of men for the best part of the way, thanks to the winter.

The cold, we are told, will take all energy out of us, and the great altitude will so rarefy the air, that we shall be unable to make the slightest muscular exertion, while the constant high wind will raise terrible tempests of snow. Such are some of the reasons given us for abandoning the enterprise, but we are obstinate, and make ready for a start.

We have three roads for approaching the Pamir, the pass of Tengez-Beï, to the south-east of Marguilane; the Terek-Davan, to the east of Osch, and the Taldik, to the south of Osch.

The only route at the present time taken by the caravans passed by the Terek-Davan. We decide not to select it, because it is the longest of the three, and as soon as we had reached Irkestame, a Russian post situated on the Chinese frontier, we should have, so to speak, to retrace our steps westward by the valley of the Alaï, until we turned southward by the Kizil-Art. Before reaching the Kizil-Art, we should find a pass about a few

BANK OF THE RIVER AT MARGUILANE.

days' march from Irkestame, that of Tuyun-Murun; but it might be snow-blocked, and with no one to aid us in getting over it, we should be exposed to one more risk of failure. Upon the other hand, the Chinese might be informed of our presence very rapidly by means of their mounted messengers, who convey to the chief of Kashgar any interesting news from the frontier, and they would send troops to stop us as soon as we set foot upon their territory beyond the lake of Kara-Kul.

So that if we went by the Terek-Davan, we should spend more

time and money, and we should risk being stopped by the warriors of the celestial empire or by the spring, which is very much to be dreaded on the Pamir plateau.

The pass of Tengiz-Beï is not far from Marguilane, and is visible from the outskirts of the town. We are told that it is always practicable, but it leads to the desert of the Alaï, which we should have to traverse for at least a week with beasts of burden. Now we have to take with us wood, forage, barley, provisions, etc., and the longer the route the more animals we shall require, and men as well. We are, in fact, in a vicious circle, for a greater number of stages means a greater quantity of provisions, to carry which there must be horses, while with more horses there must be more men to look after them, and so on. This would be a great expense, even if our means admit of organizing such a caravan, while as the route would be longer, we should reach the foot of the Kizil-Art fatigued, just when we most needed all our strength.

It is above all things necessary that those who are going right through with the enterprise should husband all their energy, and I refer to animals as well as to men.

Our base of operations must, therefore, be carried as far forward as possible; that is to say, that we must follow the shortest route and one upon which we are the best assured of finding co-operation from the inhabitants as long as there are any. But in the vicinity of the pass of Tengez-Beï, the only persons to be met with are a few Kirghiz with a very bad reputation, who would probably make off at our approach. Moreover, they are very poor and could not supply us with the forty beasts of burden we require.

There remains the Taldik route, and though it is said to be the most beset with difficulties, it is nearly opposite the pass of Kizil-Art, which is the second gate of the Pamir, and at the foot of the Taldik—to the north, of course—the Kara-Kirghiz of the Alaï have numerous winter encampments. Two of the principal khans of these tribes have come to pay a visit to the governor.

A FERGHANA WOMAN.

We have seen them, and they say that they can find us as many men and horses as we require, while one of them, Kamtchi-Beg, who inhabits Gultcha, assures us that there is not much snow in the Taldik at present. He adds, as indeed we were aware, that once we have crossed the Kara-Kul, we shall be able to follow the streams and cross the lakes upon the ice. They both advise us to avoid a certain Nazir-Sahib, a pillaging dweller in the Pamir, who will be sure to inform the Afghans if he is afraid to attack us himself. Nor must we let the Chinese post, which is probably wintering near the Rang-Kul, know of our approach, and the same with the Afghan post told off to guard the road to the Wakhan, which is wintering in the valley of the Ak-Su (Oxus).

Taking note of these warnings, we prepare to start, the first thing we do being to sell our horses, though we know that they are very sure-footed. We intend to replace them by horses of the Alaï, bred on the mountain and accustomed to its severe winters. The snow will be familiar to them, they will not be daunted by the steepest paths, and they will be easy to feed. The Alaï will have given them a foretaste of the Pamir, so to speak. We shall purchase them at Osch, where they will be brought in to us from neighbouring aouls. From Osch to the Taldik, we shall see which of them are the least likely to suit, and we shall be able to exchange these at the last moment for others.

Then, we shall arm ourselves against cold and hunger. At Marguilane we shall purchase "civilized" articles, and what we cannot get there, we shall send for to Taskhend, where we have a devoted friend in M. Müller, a Frenchman such as one would like to see many more of abroad.

Certain parts of the Pamir are uninhabitable owing to the extreme cold, and there is a scarcity of fuel. We shall have to encounter a Siberian temperature, and as in Siberia people wear felt boots over their ordinary ones, we have some made of double felt, with leather soles; the seams protected by strips of skin. We have immense stockings, reaching up to the thigh, made out of the light and supple felt of Kashgar, with trousers lined in the Kirghiz fashion, and over them a *tchalvar* (leather trousers) to protect the legs. The feet we shall protect with strips of wool, though some people advise us to use paper.

For the upper part of the body we shall have two pelisses, one of them of Kashgar sheepskin, with long wool, worn like the "bechmet" of the natives. Upon the head, a sheepskin cap coming down over the ears, and above that a "malakaï," which is like a hood of sheepskin, falling over the shoulders and fastening in front, so as to cover the whole face with the exception of the eyes, which have loopholes through the wool.

The hands will be covered with long sleeves fastened on to the end of the very ample cloak which comes down to the heels, and is called a "touloup." If with all these things on we are cold, it will be cold indeed!

For protection at night, we shall also have some thick wadded blankets, and a very close woollen blanket of European make, as a protection from the wind, with skins stretched like mattresses upon the felt which will serve as a floor.

Our house will be the double tent which we have used since the beginning of our journey, and in which five people can sleep at a push, while there is plenty of room in it for three. We shall have some iron and wooden pegs made for this tent. Rachmed and Menas do not want any tent for themselves, preferring to settle down each night among the baggage, with felt coverlets and oil-cloth in the event of bad weather. They are dressed just like us, and we all laugh heartily when we try on the many pieces of our armour.

Then we have to think about light. We shall want to be able to see well, so as to take down our notes at night, and we determine not to change our previous system, but to buy lanterns of the country, which we can protect with wooden cases. When they are broken, we can replace them with Persian lanterns made of stout oilcloth, using Russian candles in them. These lanterns will be hung from the crossbars of the tent. We do not intend to use either oil or petroleum, or to have any lamps, as in the event of a fall, the lamp is broken and the oil gets spilt, whereas if a candle is broken, the pieces can still be used.

Then we have to consider how we are to get a good fire. The only combustibles to be obtained on the plateau are roots, rough grass, and the *kisiak* (droppings of the cattle and horses), and that only at certain places. At Ak-Basoga, near the Taldik, there are a few juniper-trees along the slopes, and several of our horses will be loaded with a good provision of these, which will have to be used very carefully. But it will be necessary to be able to light a fire with speed and ease. After a hard day, the men are tired, and they are anxious to see a little fire, to warm themselves and get a cup of tea. But

A LITTLE GIRL OF THE COUNTRY.

upon the snow, with a strong wind blowing, it takes some time, even after digging a hole in the hard ground, to get a good fire. So that we must take, in addition to the tinder-boxes, the tinder, and the boxes of matches, some petroleum and spirits of wine, as well as a "hearth," or a plate of sheet iron upon which the fuel will be placed and soaked with spirits of wine before applying the match to it.

And the food, which is the capital point in every expedition, which is to the other preparations as the sun is to the planets, the base of long strategical operations, the coal of the engine, the sails of the brig, the wings of the bird! People may think me very material, and idealists may accuse me of erecting an altar to the stomach; but in reality I am erecting one to the source of all action. Readers must excuse the outspokenness of one who has often led the hard life of a traveller, and forgive his enthusiasm about the commissariat; for he has a hundred times over had occasion to mark the inevitable ill-humour, apathy and negligence of men who have been unable to restore their forces after hard work. The cistern gets empty when you keep on drawing water out and putting none in. So when we come to discuss the quantity of provisions and calculate the number of days' march, I say, when it is proposed to take food for thirty days at a pound a day, "No, let us take for forty-five days at two pounds."

But the Kirghiz assert that one does not eat nearly so much upon the Pamir as lower down, but my answer to that is, "If the provisions are in our way, we can throw them away."

And, starting from this principle, we buy sugar, salt, tea, sweetmeats, rice, smoked meat, smoked goose, smoked mutton, smoked fish from the Aral and the Ural, cheese, preserves, etc., taking double or treble the quantity considered necessary.

We have the cooking utensils repaired, and few as we have in ordinary times, we reduce our stock to the narrowest possible limits, taking only two or three saucepans of various sizes, and dishes which will do for plates as well; no forks, and only a few wooden spoons. We shall be able to get some light wooden bowls from the Kirghiz. We must not lose sight of the fact, in purchasing our material, that we shall have to carry it with us, and of two articles which can answer the same purpose, we select the one less likely to break and lighter to carry. So we take wooden shovels to clear away the snow. We also take pickaxes of various sizes, and hatchets to use upon the snow and ice.

Our medicine-chest is not a large one, but Capus, who has charge of it, fills up the gaps in it, and, thanks to the military pharmacy of the Ferghana province, we are able to get what we want. There remain the few trifling articles which we have brought from Europe to distribute among the natives whom we want to conciliate. But we have not many of them left, so we purchase at Tashkend a fine plated Winchester rifle, which we intend to give to the Khan of Kunjut, who guards the road to India upon the other side of the Pamir. A weapon so bright as this will mollify him. He is said to be cruel and barbarous,

KARA-KIRGHIZ GIRL.

and in any case he is a bad son, for he has recently had his father made away with. We shall have to get on the soft side of this young potentate. We purchase, too, some of the silk sashes of brilliant colours and picturesque patterns, which are made at Marguilane, and which are sure to be appreciated. We have also a lot of looking-glasses, rings, earrings, and other ornaments in silver and gold to give away; and we are resolved to be as polite and affable as possible all round, though it may be indispensable to show one's teeth, and have them as sharp as those of a wolf. We are, therefore, well armed, for when travelling it is advisable to hold the olive-branch in one's hand, while having a revolver in one's pocket, so as to be able to hold out the one or the other, as the occasion may require.

So we overhaul all our arms, and take a good supply of cartridges. Menas and Rachmed sharpen their swords. *Si vis pacem, etc.*

But we must be in a position to pay for any purchases we may make, or for any services which may be rendered us, and as the savages do not care much for money, of which they do not know the precise value, and which they cannot always exchange for goods, we take plenty of Turkestan khalats, with tea and sugar, of which the Kirghiz are so fond. We shall also be able to pay them with crystallized salt, which we shall get at Osch, and with powder and shot, though Rachmed says that one ought never to give that to a possible enemy.

At Osch we shall also purchase cotton stuffs made at Kashgar and bearing the Chinese customs' stamp, which is said to be the best medium of exchange. In default of cloth, the people of the Hindu-Kush, the Pamir, and the Wakhan, will also accept the silver bars called iamba, bearing the Chinese stamp. These bars, which are conical in shape, weigh one or, at the most two pounds; they are cut off as one would a stick of liquorice, and when you want to pay for anything, you chop off a bit and weigh it. The natives exchange this silver in the bazaars for goods, or have it made into trinkets, this being a mode of investing one's money which is much in favour with the savages now, as it was in the Middle Ages, when so many large monuments were profusely decorated with precious stones and minerals, while even now the wives of African chiefs often wear twenty pounds' weight of silver on them.

But it is time for me to come back to the Pamir, which is not yet crossed, and to-day (February 19th) we are still at Marguilane, waiting for a money remittance which is on the way. We soon receive the money, and at the same time comes a telegram from the chief of the Osch district, to say that snow is falling much more heavily than usual, and that the Alaï passes are blocked.

KARA-KIRGHIZ LITTLE GIRL.

We are advised to go by Tengiz-Beï, which, we are assured, will be easy to cross. But I have an instinctive mistrust of this valley of the Alaï, which we should have to pass through from end to end. I am ready to believe that it is clear of snow, when we have only got to cross it, for that is an encouragement to attempt the passage of the Pamir, the more so as in the event of the snow obstructing the route, there would be a chance of our overcoming that obstacle by a superhuman effort, but to travel from one end to the other, from Tengiz-Beï to the Kizil-Art would be to face certain failure. So to-morrow I shall make a start with Captain Grombtchefski, who has kindly offered to accompany me, and we shall see what can be done. At Osch, we shall get definite information, and I shall decide accordingly. For the matter of that, our minds are pretty well made up that we must go by the Taldik if we are to succeed, our finances scarcely admitting of our taking any other route. With enough money one can, in my opinion, go anywhere, and we have but little, so must cut our coats according to our cloth.

So we will go to Osch, and if there is one chance in ten of crossing the Taldik, we shall try our luck. The main point is to reach the Pamir quickly and without undue fatigue. Once up there, we shall travel south without looking back, just as the swimmer keeps his eyes fixed on the distant shore where he wishes to land. The first thing for us to do is to jump into the water, though the bank from which we must take off is a steep one.

We reach Osch in a tarantasse, amid a heavy fall of snow, and lose no time in getting to work. Thanks to Captain Grombtchefski, who speaks Turkish fluently and who is known to all the natives, we shall soon know all about it. The Kara-Kirghiz of the Alaï are governed by four elected chiefs, who are brothers, and whose mother is very highly esteemed by them. The election of these four chiefs has received the sanction of the Russian authorities, who entrust them with the imposition and collection of taxes. They exercise great influence over the men of their tribe, and they are very useful to us, when they come in to Osch at the summons of the Russians, who bid them procure us a guide if possible.

The four khans, who are followed by their retinue, are introduced to us, and we remark that they are all tall, with small eyes and bullet heads planted upon short necks with broad shoulders. They are dressed in pelisses and tan-coloured boots, and carry a whip in their hands. Flakes of snow are hanging about their beards and the fur of their caps, for only one of

OSCH, FROM THE THRONE OF SOLOMON.

them wears a turban, this being Batir-Beg, the eldest, who is able to read and write very easily, and who resides at Osch.

After shaking hands with them, they are provided with chairs, sitting each according to his rank, and we hold a sort of divan while cups of tea are handed round. We expound our plan for crossing the Taldik, to which they listen in silence and with a quite impassive air. Batir-Beg then points to the man sitting next to him whose eyes are almost lost in his enormous red face, and says—

"Makmud lives near the Taldik. He has seen men who

have come from there, and he will be able to tell you whether it is possible to cross it despite the *sarï-barb* (yellow snow), which has been falling for the last week."

Makmud, who is above the average height, seems quite short on account of his corpulency. He speaks with a hoarse and guttural voice, though the phrases of the vigorous and manly

MAKMUD.

Turkish language sound clear and distinct as they come from his lips.

"There is a great deal of snow on the mountain. The Taldik is blocked, but a road could be cleared and the touras taken to the other side. Only it would be necessary to wait a few days while the men were being collected, and it would take a little time to do the work. If the snow lasts we shall have a great deal of difficulty."

"Say frankly whether you think the thing is possible."

"Yes; I think so."

He then turned round to an intelligent looking man that was sitting on the fourth chair, the youngest of the party, and added—

"Mollah-Baïas is of my opinion. He knows better than I do what can be done, for he has tents at the foot of the Taldik, at Ak-Basoga."

Mollah-Baïas replied that he was of Makmud's opinion, but, he added, "we shall have great difficulty, because we are in the yellow snow season. There has been a good deal already, and there will be more. But I think that an attempt might be made."

I was overjoyed at this, as it seemed to me like opening the gate of the Pamir. We shall probably be able to cross the Taldik.

We at once began to inquire about the valley of the Alaï. No one had visited it during the winter, but they all thought that there would be some snow in it, though not very much. Batir-Beg says that it will be as well to ask the djiguite of his eldest brother, Abdullah-Khan, who fought against Skobeloff, and died in the land of Cabul, to which he had fled. Sadik, as his faithful retainer is called, accompanied him through the Pamir, Wakhan, and Badakshan; he knows the Pamir route, where he has often made baranlas in the summer. Since the death of his master, he has lived in the aoul of the second brother, Batir-Beg, and is very devoted to him.

SADIK.

Sadik, who then comes into the room, is a man with a weather-beaten face, wearing the usual sheepskin pelisse and headdress. He is a regular Kara-Kirghiz, and there is a look of suspicion in his small eyes. He kneels, without saying a word, close to Makmud till his opinion is asked, when he says that he has never seen the Alaï in winter, but he presumes that it can be traversed.

"And how about the pass of Kizil-Art, which is to the south-east of the Taldik, and which leads to the Pamir?"

"I have heard it said by Kirghiz from the Pamir that it is always open."

"And on the Pamir?"

"I am told that there is not much snow."

If all this is true, things look very promising. The conversation then continues.

"How long will it take, should you imagine, to reach a spot where we shall find a little brushwood and last year's grass?"

"You are speaking of Basaï-Gumbaz, at the source of the Ak-Su (the Oxus)."

"Yes."

"In twelve days, from the foot of the Taldik, from the Alaï."

"And you, Batir-Beg?"

"A fortnight."

"And you, Makmud?"

"Three weeks, for you have baggage, and the season is very much against you."

The captain takes Batir-Beg's view, while I agree with Makmud, and in my inmost heart I believe that, making allowances for the incidents of the route, we shall be a good month before we reach a village, and perhaps longer. So we must take our precautions accordingly.

Sadik having consented to show us the way, I ask him how far he knows the road. He says—

"As far as the Wakhan. You wish to go by the Kunjut. I have never been in that country. When you reach the Wakhan after travelling westward for several days, you turn to the left about noon in order to get to the Kunjut."

"Have you heard talk of the people of that country?"

"I know that they come on to the Pamir during the summer to steal the flocks and to carry off the men."

This ends the conference, and Batir-Beg promises to bring us the next day a memorandum of what he considers indispensable for crossing the Pamir as far as Basaï-Gumbaz, calculated for eight persons.

For it is best to reckon upon everything going badly, and upon our encountering almost insurmountable difficulties until we are upon the Pamir, beyond the Kizil-Art. Further on, these difficulties will diminish, at least so far as regards the snow. For we are told that there is no snow upon the Pamir, and if this is not quite accurate, at all events there cannot be much. As to the Alaï, we are told that there is "only a little," and we will call that "a good deal." It is evident, therefore, that the early stages will be the most difficult, so that we must, as far as possible, lighten the task then.

Batir-Beg thinks that the passage of the Taldik will necessitate the employment of a hundred men on horse and on foot. We shall let them do the rough part of the work, and then send them back, directing our efforts mainly to not fatiguing the men and horses which have got to go the whole way. They must travel in comfort as far as the Alaï, and this category comprises Sadik and two Kirghiz whom he is going to employ, Menas, Rachmed, and ourselves. Till we get beyond the Kizil-Art, on the other side of the Alaï, we shall employ another band of about forty Kirghiz with their horses which will convey our baggage, so that our own horses, with no load to carry, will arrive comparatively fresh upon the Pamir. Upon reaching the lake of Kara-Kul, we shall send back the second squad of the Kirghiz, and shall then be left to our own resources. It will also be after leaving Kara-Kul that we shall begin to use our provisions, unless anything unforeseen occurs, so that this lake will be practically our starting-point. Such, at least, are our plans, though they may, of course, be subject to alteration when we reach the scene of operations.

In the meanwhile we continue our purchases of horses, and I telegraph to my companions, who have stayed behind at Marguilane with Rachmed, to come on as soon as they have all ready.

Two days after this, our whole party was assembled at the house of Colonel Deibner, who offered us the most cordial hospitality, with the exception of Rachmed, who was following on with the baggage. When he arrives all will be ready and we shall start.

We have an immense number of small slabs of bread mixed with fat and baked twice over. Then we have mutton boiled down and salted and placed in bladders, where it will keep for a long time owing to the cold. We shall only use it in critical circumstances, or when we are unable to light a fire, either from want of fuel, or want of time, or from the violence of the wind. At Ak-Basoga we shall find some sheep, and it will be easy to freeze their flesh, which, if kept away from the light, will not go bad.

Then we prepare flour and bread-cakes without any fat, while we have some millet seed roasted which we shall be able either to have cooked or to take in our pocket and munch as we go along. For our stages will be lengthy ones, making it impossible for us to halt except for the night, and at great altitudes one wants to eat not much at a time, but frequently. This is why the corpulent Makmud advises us to add to our cargo about sixty pounds of dried apricots, which we can suck *en route* if we feel a sinking at the stomach. Moreover, the Kirghiz are very partial to dried apricots, as, for the matter of that, we are.

We buy some oil which will be a substitute occasionally for mutton fat, which will serve us instead of butter, and which we have salted before starting. The bread, too, has rather more than the ordinary quantity of salt in it, for the success of the expedition, which necessitates a great physical effort, depends upon the state of the stomach. Every now and then sweetmeats will be distributed among the eight men of the regular army, so we shall have our little luxuries.

The horses will have a pack-saddle, and clothing of double felt, which will cover them from head to tail at night, and which will be folded up during the day time. The shoes, nails, hammers, rasps, and all the other blacksmith's tools, together with the needles for sewing the felt, and the string, are carefully packed up. We buy, too, some Russian ropes made of flax, as they are much stronger than the natives' ropes, though we also take a lot of woollen and horsehair ropes made by the Kirghiz, as they are more supple to handle in frosty weather, and are more readily cut, which is very important when horses step in the snow and one's hands are too numbed to untie a knot. I will not mention the minor articles, for the reader may think that I have entered too much into detail, though I have mentioned all these points to show how complicated our preparations were, and that there is this in common between a journey of this kind and war, that both must be undertaken with prudence and boldly executed.

To-day (March 5th) all is ready except the barley, which Makmud has undertaken to deliver to us at Ak-Basoga, at the foot of the Taldik. As we proceed, Sadik will secure the assistance of one of his friends, who belongs to the tribe of Makmud. The eighth person will be an individual who has inhabited the

Pamir, and who is expected at once. Captain Grombtchefski has gone back to Marguilane, after having lent us all the assistance in his power; for which we are very grateful to him. The sub-commander of the district, Captain Gluchanovski, will accompany us as far as Ak-Basoga, and his presence will facilitate our passage of the Taldik, by securing for us the genuine assistance of the Kara-Kirghiz, who are not the most obedient men in the world.

We start to-morrow, and we send a farewell telegram of thanks to our good friend Müller at Tashkend, to the Governor-General, and to Generals Ivanoff and Karalkoff, who reply to wish us "Godspeed." Why should we not succeed, after all? We have quite made up our minds to persevere to the end. We hope that in case of failure our compatriots will not be the first to cast stones at us, and that if we succeed they will not blame us for our hardihood.

March 6th.

At last we are in the saddle. We lose sight of Osch, and are in the mountain, glad to be really off and with the sensation of being about to realize a project long contemplated. If only the cup does not slip from our lips just as we are beginning to taste it.

We pass along parallel with the spurs of the Alaï as far as Madi, and the road reminds us of the environs of Saridjuï, with its bare hills so characteristic of Central Asia. At Madi we sleep under the tent, and so resume the camping-out life, with the fires, the picketing of horses, and the coming and going of our men.

On the 7th of March, we reach Kaflan-Kul, which lies in a hollow shut in by mountains. As we ascend, the snow is thicker, and on the following day we descend by a pass which is slippery with melting snow into another and much larger depression, where there is green grass, upon which the flocks and herds are feeding, close beneath the walls of the small fort of Gultcha.

To the east we see the tents of the portly Makmud, who is to join our troop. The fort is commanded by Captain Galberg, who lives there with his wife and two children. He has a charming family, and does not in the least mind the solitude.

At Gultcha, Sadik presents to us a man named Abdu-Rasoul, who will be quite willing to follow us. He is a handsome and brawny Kara-Kirghiz, very tall and about thirty years of age. This is the last point at which we shall be in contact with the

NADI.

Russians, so we overhaul our equipment, to see that we are not short of anything. The horses rest all day on the 9th, and we give them plenty of sound hay and oats. This is their last good meal, and we, too, take advantage for the last time of the excellent Russian hospitality extended to us by Captain Galberg. These are incidents in life not readily forgotten. A Kashgar man who is out of employment offers us his services, and tells Rachmed, who takes a great fancy to him, that he knows how to load horses, and will follow us to the end of the world. Our volunteer, it may be added, plays the *domburak* (a stringed instrument) very well, has a good voice and can tell a number of interesting stories. He is full of ardour, but he must either be a humbug or cannot realize what he is undertaking to do. To-morrow will show, as a single stage will suffice to prove of what stuff he is made.

March 10th.

In the rain and the snow we arrive by a fairly good road, passing through scenery which reminds us of Ablatum and the Caucasus,

GULTCHA.

at Kizelkurgane, which is a reduced likeness of Gultcha. It takes its name from the red fragments of the walls of a ruined fortress, which the ancient khans of the Ferghana had built as a residence for a squad of *zakketches* (custom-house men), who were kept there to collect dues from the caravans, and for soldiers who were told off to look out for the horse-stealers (*barantachis*).

In the evening, Rachmed comes to us with a long face to say that the Kashgar singer has disappeared.

THE PAMIR. 59

March 11th.

The cold commences. At 8 a.m., the thermometer is two or three degrees below freezing point, and the snow is falling, with a light breeze from the north-north-west.

We pass through the narrow defile of Djangrik, which is very wild and picturesque, with steep overhanging rocks, and we are shown upon a plateau just in front of it the ruins of a fortress supposed to have been built by the Chinese.

Following the river, we arrive at Sufi-Kurgane, where we meet Batir-Beg, who has just come back from the Taldik. He tells us that the snow is very deep, that it will take at least three days to clear a path, and that there is considerable danger of avalanches. The snow is still falling, and in the Terek-Davan Pass ten horses have been swept away by an avalanche. This is bad news, and we wonder whether it will be possible to get through, though perhaps Batir-Beg wants to make us pay more for the service of the Kirghiz.

ABDL-RASOUL.

At Sufi-Kurgane, the road branches off towards the Terek-Davane and Kashgar, where the Chinese are waiting for us, as we have given notice of our coming.

March 12th.

The weather is bad, a strong south wind driving in our faces, and the snow falling in blinding storms. When it stops we find that there is so much that our horses sink up to the stirrups. The sun comes out, and the wind does not drop; so, nearly blinded by the reflection and the cold air, we make a bend by the kichlak of Tchulakbuz, passing close by a well-worn path without seeing it, and finally reaching the tents which have been put up for us at Ak-Basoga, at the foot of the Taldik. Batir-Beg informs us that he has collected a number of men, and that they will begin to clear the pass in the morning, as soon as the scouts return.

Every one is agreed, and we can quite believe them, that the pass is blocked with an enormous quantity of snow.

We are at an altitude of about ten thousand feet, and the cold begins to be very severe, while at Marguilane the heat is quite trying.

We do not so much mind the cold, but the snow! It is the one subject of conversation with us, and we more than ever regret that the slow rate at which our preparations were made prevented us starting in February, as we had wished to do.

March 13th.

We get the barley delivered to us, and the Kirghiz advance into the defile of the Taldik. Some men who came back at night say that they will be through the pass to-morrow. The sky is clear, and there is no wind. If this weather lasts five or six days, it will be possible to work, and we shall get through, if only the wind does not get up. The variations of temperature are very great, for at 9 a.m. the thermometer marks 75° F. in the sun and 10° F. below freezing in the shade, while at 2 p.m. it is nearly 100° F. in the sun and three degrees below freezing in the shade; at 6 p.m. there are eighteen degrees of frost, while at 9.20 p.m. the glass is several degrees below zero.

There is no wind, and the sky is cloudy eastward.

We ask for fifteen horses to be sent from Sufi-Kurgane, for at Tchulakbuz we shall only have fifteen for carrying the baggage

to the Kara-Kul, all the rest being employed to trample down the snow.

March 14th.

When I wake up at daybreak, I look through the opening in the curtain of the tent, and I see a dazzling white space before me. It will be a very serious matter if this is snow, but as my eyes get accustomed to the light, I see that the surface of the ground is lighted up by the radiation, so when Sadik enters to light the fire, I have quite a cheerful face.

At 7 a.m., the temperature is not much above zero, with very little wind; at noon there are several degrees of frost in the shade, while the thermometer is about sixty in the sun.

Makmud tells us that among the men at work in the Taldik pass is one whose tribe lives on the Pamir, and who has his wife and children here. He is willing to accompany us, and will get us guides up there if possible.

We kill three sheep, and buy about sixty-five pounds more flour for gruel, and four hundred pounds for our attendants as far as the Kara-Kul. We have nearly a ton of barley. We reckon upon losing several horses, and we shall feed the others better.

At night, there is no wind, but the sky is clear. This is just what we want, and at 8.15 p.m. there are nearly thirty degrees of frost, which will be our salvation.

At that hour, Batir-Beg says that to-morrow we shall be able to send the luggage on upon thirty horses. At a distance of about twelve miles, there are three avalanches which threaten danger, so that it will be necessary to encamp beyond them, therefore we shall have to start to-morrow before daylight. We are told that the Kirghiz of the Pamir who is to accompany us says that he formerly inhabited the Kunjut, and traded there, so that we could not have a better guide. In answer to our questions about the Alaï, the natives can only say that it looks very white in the distance, but it will be time enough to think of that after we have crossed the Taldik.

The barometer is rising, the sky is of an azure blue, and we are all sanguine, while I am personally very pleased at having selected this route. Going out of the tent to look at the thermometer, I find, at 9.30 p.m., that it is four degrees below zero, with no wind. By Allah! I believe that we shall get through, though it is well not to be too certain.

We are encamped at the extreme end of a *cul-de-sac* formed by mountains with sharp peaks covered with snow; the stars are shining, and the light which filters through the tent is very poetical,

SATTI-KUL.

while poetical, too, are the barkings of the dogs, the sound of the horses feeding in their mangers, the crackling of the wood under the bellows, the white expanse beyond, and even the deep bass voice of Menas singing a Turkish war song as he mends a hood.

March 15th.

The man who is supposed to have been a trader in the Kunjut is brought for us to see. He is a curious sort of trader—a short little man, very broad and fat, with an enormous face, suffering from anastomasis and unable to look at the fire, and very dirty. He is willing to go with us if we will pay him well. He belongs to the Teit horde of the Ichkilik tribe, who live near the Rang-Kul. He does not quite know why he has come to the Alaï, but he has been very well treated there, for he belongs to the great family of the Kara-Kirghiz.

We put several questions to him, and his answers show that

DEPOT FOR CROSSING THE TAMIR.

he knows the road very well. We ask him if there is much snow up there, and he says that God alone knows. He evidently will not commit himself. He will go on foot and remain among his people for the rest of the winter, returning in the summer to Ak-Basoga.

The fine weather continues, so we put on the Pamir dress to be photographed in, and very queer we look with the enormous cloaks and boots, which give us the appearance of so many antediluvians. With our spectacles and the hoods drawn down over our noses, our heads look as if they were in a diving dress, while there are so many arms in our tent that Rachmed says it is like a barrack.

KUMGANE AND TCHILIM.

Before sunset, the baggage is sent off, and an effort will be made to get it to Taldik without a halt, the workmen who have been trampling down the snow assisting the *kiraketches* (muleteers). At the hour when the mollah calls to prayer, Makmud will come and call us, so we settle our accounts, give away some presents, and have a long conversation with Captain Gluchanovski as we sip our tea. Then we write a few letters, and so to bed.

There is a fall of snow, but it is not heavy. Up till nearly midnight, I can hear Rachmed telling stories to our men and those of the Russian captain, with intervals of song accompanied by the domburak. The men are smoking and drinking, and I can hear the gurgle of the *tchilim* (water-pipe). Then the anecdotes begin afresh, broken by the mocking laugh of Menas, who is a sceptic, while Rachmed can draw the long-bow. Menas stops laughing, having doubtless gone off to sleep, and I follow his example.

It would be as well if our men would do the same, but it is customary to enjoy one's self with friends before undertaking a long journey. I wonder whether ours will be a prosperous one! Allah alone can tell, as the hideously ugly guide named Satti-Kul would say.

EQUIPPED FOR THE ROUTE.

CHAPTER XI.

THE PAMIR (*continued*).

The start for the Taldik—Saying good-bye—Going through the pass—The valley of the Taldik—Bad news from the Alaï—No more assistants—Preparing for the combat—Another world—Where are we?—In the snow—The struggle—The "White Sea"—Polar scenery—On the way to Urtak—Shepherds hemmed in by snow—The troop loses heart—A rest—Scaling the Kizil-Art—Upon "the roof of the world"—At last!

"ALLAH is great!" drawls the mollah, as he announces the hour of prayer. It is time to get up, and, upon looking at my watch and finding that it is a quarter to three, I call out to Rachmed and Menas, and tell them to light the fire and make some tea. This is soon done, and my companions awake in their turn, while I go out to consult the weather. The sky is clouding over, and there is no wind, with about twenty-six degrees of frost. Let us hope that this fine weather will last. I see a very burly figure coming towards me along the path traced in the snow, and this proves to be Makmud, who is very much wrapped up, and who has come to wake us. Captain Gluchanovski, Batir-Beg, and Mollah-Païus, the nephew, come up soon afterwards, and, seated on the felt, we drink our tea while waiting for the rising of the moon. The horses are eating a final wisp or two of hay, and some are being loaded with wood, and will be sent on under the supervision of Sadik, who will have Abdur-Rasul and Satti-Kul under his orders. The others are the horses without a load, which are to be sent on ahead of us, so that there may be no risk of any delay, while they will also make it better travelling for us by treading down the snow.

They are ready about 4.30 a.m, and we go out of the tent to see them start. How lovely the moon looks, and how gracefully she stands out in the firmanent, not seeming nearly so far off as the astronomers calculate her to be.

Satti-Kul, who is not at all expansive, is the first to start, and he does so without saying a word, with a stick in his hand and leading a horse, which half the others will follow of their own accord. We have purposely left them at liberty, as they will not lose themselves so much, and the fall of one will not entail that of the horse in front of or behind him. This first batch will be followed by Abdur-Rasul, who will stimulate the lazy horses by his shouts.

Abdur-Rasul has several acquaintances among the people present, and he says good-bye to Makmud, his khan, before starting. His adieu is a very brief one, consisting of stroking his beard with his hand, and exclaiming, " God is great ! " Sadik is more loquacious. He reproaches Batir-Beg for having drawn him into this expedition. " You know that I had not sown my barley. Why do you send me up into the snow? How can you tell if I shall come back? You will look after my business during my absence?"

Batir-Beg smiles and tells him to make his mind easy. Sadik has girthed his last horse while he has been talking. He repeats his favourite phrase of "Allah is great!" whistles and strokes each horse on the quarter as it goes by, the whole of them going along in Indian file, with Sadik bringing up the rear.

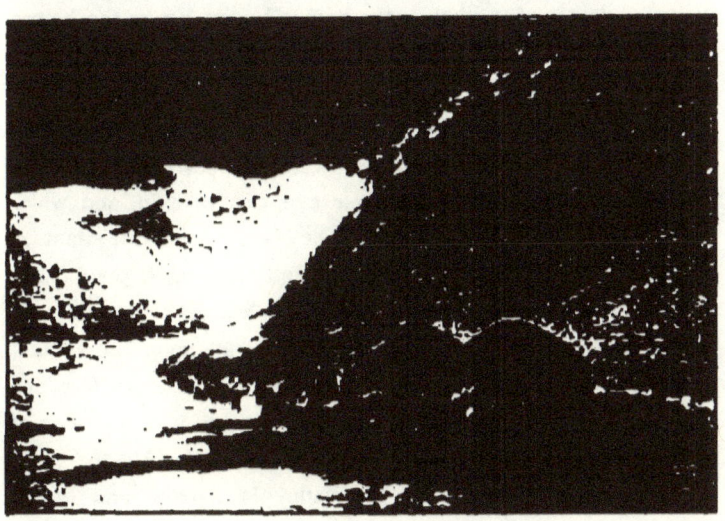

STARTING FOR THE TALDIK.

We return to the tent in order to breakfast with the captain, and then we don our harness and get on our horses, preceded by Mollah-Paias. The khans raise their hands to their beards, and the captain exclaims, "God be with you! God bless you! Au revoir! Good health and good luck!"

We return the compliment, and then start, turning back in the saddle to have a last look, and waving our whips until we come to the defile which leads to the pass of Taldik.

At first there is not more than three feet of snow, and it is pretty hard, owing to the frost. Then the ascent begins, and we clamber over the rocks. There is no snow on the slopes, and the frost, which down below had been a help, here becomes an obstacle, for it has made the rock very slippery, and our horses, sure-footed as they are, fall about. Their falls are not very dangerous, however, as there is a thick covering of moss on the rock. We have to make frequent stoppages to let the horses gain breath, and then the ascent begins again, the horses, with heads down and dilated nostrils, clinging to the asperities of the soil. The soil in many places gives beneath their feet, the hard crust breaks through, or a stone slips from under their hoofs, and so they mount to the ascent nervously, as if stricken with fear at the void which their eye can take in, and which they feel to be behind them. They stop short for want of breath, with their legs stretched out and quite stiff, their flanks heaving with fatigue. What stout, good beasts!

At eight o'clock, we eat a crust of bread upon the summit of the Taldik, at an altitude of about twelve thousand feet, and the next thing is to find a way out of the narrow valley of the same name which leads to the plateau of the Alaï.

We follow a ridge, for the valley is narrow and buried beneath masses of snow, amid which a horseman would disappear. Quartz rocks are seen emerging from this mass of snow, as well as the summits of buildings buried beneath it. We then leave this ridge which divides the valley, descending as it were a steep roof, and at the bottom we come upon a succession of regular wells, the site of which is marked by groups of Kirghiz at rest, who hoist the baggage on to the horses, and wade through the snow with heavy trunks on their backs, one of them pulling the carrier in front and another pushing him from behind. We have several falls. When one man falls into the snow, the others set to hauling him out, and when that is done they extricate his horse. We pass the pack-horses one after the other, and it is a question when they will overtake us. They have been on the march since 4 a.m., and yesterday they did not halt till midnight. In places there are over six feet of snow, and nowhere have the horses less than up to their necks.

At ten o'clock, we take refuge upon a stony ridge which has been swept by the wind. We shall feel the cold very much, but we shall be free from the avalanches. We clear away the snow, and settle down as best we can. As the men arrive, they take their places above or below us, and the poultry are placed upon perches, out of the way of the foxes. The sun comes out strong and begins to scorch us, there being ninety-five degrees at eleven o'clock. The first pack-horse arrives at 1.20 p.m., and the snow begins to fall, the rest of the muleteers coming in soon after. They leave the baggage on the pathway, so that it looks like the *débris* of a routed army, this being done so that it may be easier to reload, and there are no robbers to be feared in this desolate country. The horses are got together to take them down to drink at the stream, where a hole has been made in the ice, and also for fear of wolves at night.

At four o'clock, the snow is falling fast, but it stops at 5.30 p.m., and there is no wind, with about twenty degrees of frost. At nightfall, a part of the footmen, who had been sent on in front, came and encamped above us, grouped around Mollah-Païus, their chief. At midnight, there were about thirty-eight degrees of frost.

March 17th.

During the night, an easterly wind began to blow with great violence, and at 5 a.m. there were thirty-eight degrees of frost in the tent, and rather more outside. Our men, worn out with fatigue, are asleep, and it is useless to wake them up and hurry the departure. We cannot take advantage of the snow being frozen, for the ropes cannot be handled in the dark, and it is impossible to load the iouks or to secure them. We must wait for the sun to thaw the ropes and the limbs of the men, which are numbed by the cold and bitter east wind.

The sun will melt the snow, but what is to be done then? Rachmed has been bleeding from the nose, and he had a violent headache all day yesterday.

We all have spangles of ice upon our hair and beards; and from our noses, which are very red, issues a sort of vapour, which at once condenses and drops on to my pocket-book, punctuating what I write with small bits of ice. These stops of a new kind are quite useless, for I write in hieroglyphics, which will have to be deciphered afterwards.

To the east, above the pass of the Taldik, we see two white peaks, behind which is concealed a sun which shines for some other world, no doubt, as he bestows upon us only a very pale sort of light, and I wonder whether he is not going out altogether. That would be a very striking contrast with the previous twenty-four hours. But in due course his rays shine above the mountains, and we are delighted to put on our spectacles, and to descend into the valley, where we march along under the shade of the mountain. At seven o'clock, we make a start, and resolve to encamp this evening at the end of the hollow of the Taldik. We descend one steep path and ascend another, finally coming down into a broader valley and marching upon the ice of the winding stream. We choose the places where there is not much snow, and take care to keep clear of the avalanches. We often leave the river, where in some places there is not more than eighteen inches of snow, which reassures the horses, who have not forgotten their experience of the day before.

THE FIRST ENCAMPMENT UPON THE OTHER SIDE OF THE TALDIK PASS.

It is to our left that the snow is dangerous, for it has accumulated in the ravines and gorges, and the rocks have caught immense balls of snow, which hang over the road and present a most alarming appearance. So we do not talk much, but keep our eyes fixed on them as we ride along. We come upon a troop of fifty Kirghiz squatting upon the side of a rock, munching a bit of bread and resting before going back to Ak-Basoga. They are the rear-guard of the band of labourers who have prepared the road for us. Their leader tells us that it is ready as far as the Alaï. I ask him if there is much snow in the Alaï, and he stretches out his hand first in the direction of the pass and then in that of the Alaï, saying, "Barabar! barabar!" which means that it is the same. This is a bad piece of news.

Mirza-Païas takes us to encamp in a well-sheltered gorge situated to the right of the road, where we are to wait for our iouks. The wind has cleared away the snow, and the spot is a pleasant one, the sun shining, and the thermometer marking eighty-four degrees.

Rachmed is in a good humour and begins to sing, whereas last night he was lugubrious and said that we should all perish. He has regained courage, and said to me in a very serious tone, "I feel that we shan't die." And then he began to sing a song of victory over the Taldik, while to-morrow we shall enter upon the valley of the Alaï. I send Sadik and five or six Kirghiz to reconnoitre the "positions of the enemy," for some of our men have said that from this point the snow will not be so deep. Our scouts will bring us in word about this before sunset.

Sadik comes back first, and is followed by the others, all of them using the same Turkish expression, which I do not believe that I shall ever forget: "Barabar! barabar!" ("It is the same thing"). They say this in a most doleful tone and shake their heads.

They look straight at us, watching the impression which this may make on us, and as much as to say, "What will you decide to do?" They no doubt hope that we shall turn back. In truth, the news is very serious, for we shall not have the help of the natives. Who will trace out our route for us? And we shall have no one to feel the way for us. We shall have to sound our way, like a navigator in unknown waters.

Some of the Kirghiz who have been working in the trenches of the Taldik are already on the way to their tents, and we are going to send back the others, as they are very fatigued. I see that they are lying outstretched in the sun, so fast asleep that it is almost impossible to wake them. We make presents to their chiefs, cordially thank Mollah-Païas, give him the remainder of the sum out of which he had received half in advance, and entrust him with a friendly message for General Karalkoff. He and his followers disappear down the gorge just as the last of the packhorses come up, so tired that they drop before they are unloaded.

I mount upon a rock close to our encampment, and from the summit of it I can overlook the ridges which shelter us and can make out the chains of the Alaï and the Trans-Alaï like two fragments of chaos. Before my eyes, I can see nothing but white, and feel like one cast upon some other planet. I can make out, too, the hills of the valley of the Alaï, intertwined like the white shields of warriors at the foot of the immense and impassable peaks of the Trans-Alaï, the second rampart of the Pamir.

In whatever direction the eye looks, all is white; there is, as it were, an immaculate shroud spread over this lifeless nature. One might fancy one's self in some accursed land, abandoned by its inhabitants, who had quitted it for some better world.

To-morrow, we shall make a plunge into this unknown world, the gloomy landscapes of which seem to be quietly making game of us.

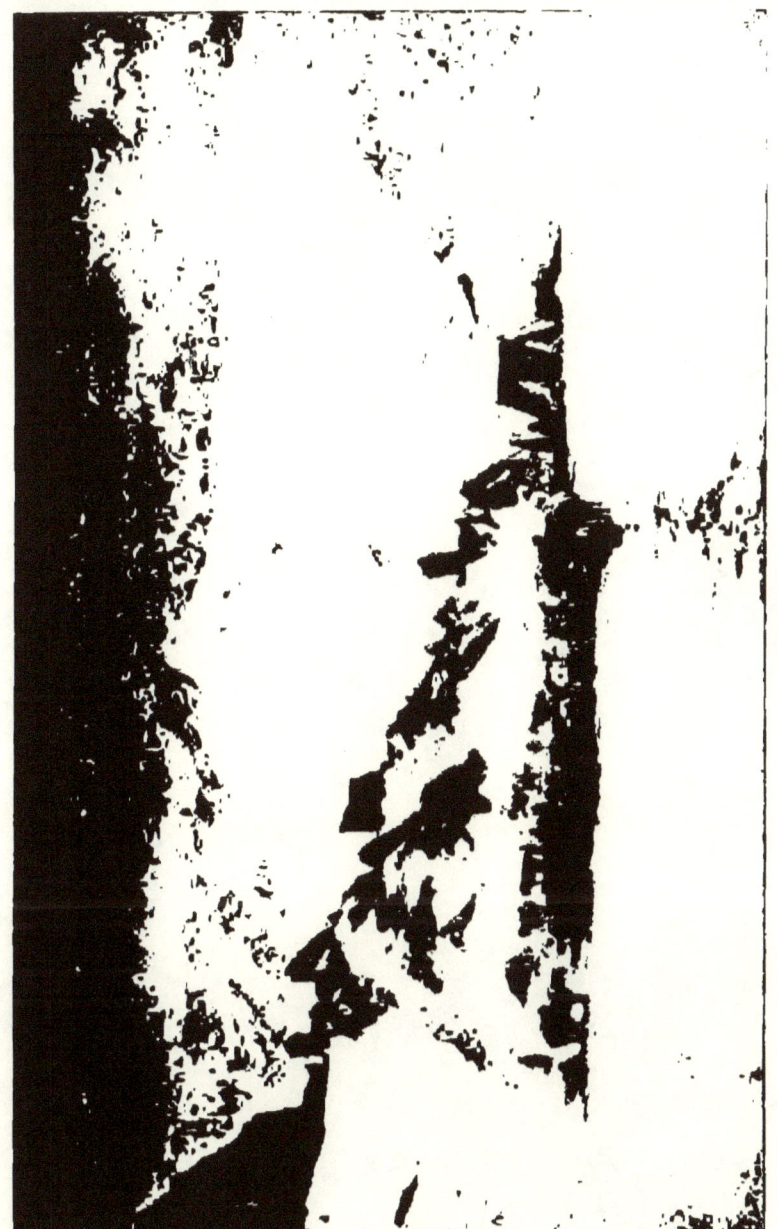

ENCAMPMENT AT FAIPUR.

We have left about fifty horses and twenty men, who must go with us to the Pamir. They will carry our baggage and our provisions, which we shall then put on to the twenty reserve horses confided to the five men of our regular forces which are specially told off to look after them.

We have had two most trying days, and we can foresee that to-morrow will be not less so, and each one of us is preparing for the trial.

Several already have chapped lips, sore eyes, and frost-bitten cheeks. The natives adopt the following precautions; they apply to their skin the leaves of a cactus which is only found in the Alaï during the summer, and they have a bag full of these leaves with them. They also make themselves a special kind of spectacle with horsehair, placing a wad of it under their sheepskin cap, and letting it drop down over their eyes, which it protects from the reflection. As to their cheeks, they just smear them over with mud or horse-dung. Thus these Kirghiz, who are not at the best of times very handsome, present the appearance of demons, or of Mongol figure-heads which have designedly been made very ugly.

KARA-KIRGHIZ.

What a pity we cannot leave our encampment to-morrow before sunset, and utilize the frost which makes the snow so hard! But this is impossible, owing to the ropes getting frozen during the night and being as hard as wood in the morning. The horses will not be loaded until late, and they will reach the valley of the Alaï when it has already got warm and the snow is becoming soft, so the difficulties will be very great, perhaps insurmountable.

March 19th.

We start with Sadik and two very active Kirghiz, who are well acquainted with the Alaï. Menas also forms part of the advance guard. Abdur-Rasul, Rachmed, and Satti-Kul follow, with twenty horses not loaded, behind them coming the thirty loaded horses and their conductors.

We follow the course of the river, which is so frozen that we can travel over the ice, and we make our way without much difficulty out of the valley of the Taldik. We are then upon the plateau of the Alaï, which extends from west to east, and our eyes have been so tried by the heat and cold that we cannot distinguish the end of it.

Before us is the grandest or at all events the most dazzling of spectacles. To the north is the barrier of the Alaï; to the south, the Kauffman peak (22,000 feet) and the Kizil-Aguin (21,400 feet) emerge from the chain of the Trans-Alaï. Snow covers everything except the smooth sides of the rocks, upon which it has no hold. The day is a very fine one, and the plain extends like a river between two very steep banks, while it is so dazzlingly bright, owing to the radiation, that the sky seems dull by comparison. At our feet, the snow sparkles so that it seems as if there was a flood of light running along the surface of the soil, and as if the stars, after having been by some magical process reduced to diamond dust, with flashes of gold, had been sprinkled about upon this stream of light.

It is through this radiation of fiery heat in the sun, and of ice in the shade, that we have to make our way. As long as we are marching parallel with the spurs of the Alaï, things are not so bad, as there is little more than three feet of snow. But at length we are obliged to strike due south, through the valley, where there is not, of course, a single path to be seen. We discuss a moment, and decide to make straight for the river of Kizil-Art; it flows into the Alaï, not far from the pass which leads up to the Pamir. We shall have to feel our way, picking out the places where there is the least snow, so that the horses which have a load on their backs may be able to proceed.

CROSSING THE ALAI.

So we advance along the snow, Sadik, with his instinct of a savage, leading the way. For half an hour we get on all right, but the horse ridden by Sadik suddenly sinks into the soft snow, and despite the skill of the rider and the free use of the whip, he cannot find his legs. Sadik is unable to extricate himself till we come to his help, and to that of his mount. This is a recommencement of the series of falls and mishaps of the previous days.

The lead is then assumed alternately by Sadik and the two Kirghiz, and the leader takes his pelisse off, throws it over his horse, which he leads by the bridle, and with his long staff feels his way like a blind man. This does not prevent us from following him in full confidence, and we have to go a roundabout way, which lengthens the journey very much, for we scarcely seem to get any nearer to the Trans-Alaï. which we expected to reach in no time. We advance at the rate of twenty or perhaps only ten paces a minute, though when upon a ridge we may perhaps accomplish sixty. We are frequently compelled to come to a dead stop.

We are all of us exhausted and out of breath, devoid of all strength, and nearly blind. We have splitting headaches and a feeling of suffocation. One man is stretched out on his back, close beside his horse, which is lying on its side; another man is asleep as he stands with his head resting against the saddle; a third is whipping his poor horse, to the tail of which he clings like a drowning man to a buoy. Some of the men were bleeding from the nose, and so were the horses, the blood freezing as it trickled down their muzzles, and looking like ruby stones. They also had clots of frozen blood on their bodies.

One horse nearly fell into a hole, and he had to be pulled out as if he was dead, with ropes passed under his belly. Then two or three girths snapped and had to be mended. If a pack-horse falls, he has to be unloaded, and it is no easy matter to untie the knots in the shade (there were nine degrees of frost at noon), for they are covered with ice and our hands are numbed. So the ropes have to be cut, the horse is got on to his legs, and the boxes or bales are again placed on his back. Sometimes they have to be carried on the men's backs, after a way has been cleared for them with shovels, as the snow is more than six feet deep everywhere. Poles higher than any of us are pushed in and disappear.

After having got through this difficult bit of ground, we rest awhile. We hardly know which direction to take, for there is nothing to show that one is better than another, the snow being literally trackless and almost exasperating in its inert and, as it were, indifferent expanse. It seems to irritate the very animals, and if perchance a wolf has left any trace, we follow it as long as we can, like a thread of Ariadne, in a labyrinth of our own tracing. This track leads us to some dead wall, or rather to some hole, and so we have to beat back again. At last we determine to go in the direction of the Kizil-Art, and have to drag along in the crumbling snow.

Our caravan is dotted about over the plain like the beads of a broken chaplet. The black beads agglomerate wherever a horse or his rider have fallen and stopped the progress of those who follow in his track.

And this goes on from 8 a.m. to 4.30 p.m. without any rest. We had no place to halt at, and so we go on till we are fairly spun out. On the way, we share a little bread with our mounts, eat a dried apricot, and munch some roasted millet, which gives us stamina to go on till we reach the declivity upon which we intend to encamp.

With a shovel or two we clear away the snow, and then the felt is spread out, the tent put up, and the fire lighted with spirits of wine. The tea and the millet porridge are got ready for us and for the hungry men who drop in one by one. The poor horses, tethered near the tent after their girths have been loosed, paw up the snow with their hoofs to try and get at the wretched grass and roots buried beneath it.

The whole caravan will not be got together before night-time. The sun has just sunk behind the mountains, a long way off, in the direction of France, that is, to the west of us. We are still

ENCAMPMENT ON THE ALAÏ, OPPOSITE PEAK KAUFFMANN.

waiting for two or three horses, which are now within a hundred paces of us, and it is seven o'clock before we have all had our porridge and tea, and the horses their small allowance of barley. They are now ranging around the three small mounds where we are encamped, or rather they are swimming, so to speak, around the islets upon which we have taken refuge from the inundation.

The breeze is from the south-south-east. The summits of the Trans-Alaï become wrinkled with clouds, the peaks display their plumes, and the firmament shines over our heads with the splendour of one which had just been turned brand-new out of chaos. The snow has disappeared from our gaze with the sun, and the blue vault seems to soar higher than heaven itself above this polar desert, amid which our three small fires flicker like so many rush candles in an immense banqueting hall.

At 8 p.m., there are sixty-eight degrees of frost.

At six in the morning, there were seventy-five, and we have all slept badly—have felt as if we were being suffocated; our bedclothes have seemed to weigh us down, we have felt pains in our heads, a singing in our ears, a smarting of the lips and eyes, etc.

We could not get to sleep at all. If we heaped the clothing on our bodies we were warm, but had a feeling of oppression; while if we threw them off, we were all of a shiver. If so much as the nose was exposed to the air, it was at once frost-bitten. So we passed the night, alternately burying ourselves beneath the clothes and putting our heads out to breathe, just like a duck which sees a gunner coming and plunges beneath the surface, bobbing up its head every now and again.

Before sunrise, all is still in the camp. The men, huddled one against the other, are as motionless as so many bales. The horses, coated with ice and standing motionless, look as if they were petrified. The stars are no longer visible, and the whole landscape looks as if it had been hewn out of an immense block of camphor. Can it be that we have got stranded, like some Robinson of the ice, at the entrance of a "White Sea," of which the plateau forms the channel?

The sun rises, and his warm rays thaw men and horses alike. The horses begin to move, and the men emerge from beneath their rugs, the warmth unloosing their tongues just as it makes the ropes more supple and enables us to prepare for a fresh start. We must try and reach the river of Kizil-Aguin as quickly as possible, in the hope that its frozen floor will not have too thick a carpet of snow. We shall follow the ridges as much as possible, for the surface undulates a good deal near the river, which has very high banks.

After eating some meat, we leave at 9.15 a.m. As far as the Kizil-Aguin there is a repetition of the falls, etc., which occurred the previous day, and it is 3 p.m. when we descend a ravine which brings us to the level of the river. Sadik, who is leading the way, puts his horse into a trot to show us that the road is good, there being only two feet of loose snow upon a hard bottom, so we might fancy ourselves in a riding-school. Abdur-Rasul, who is with us to-day, calls out to those who have not come down, "Ioul iakche!" ("Good road!"), and then sets up a song of triumph.

All goes well for three parts of an hour, but at a bend of the river the wind has drifted the snow to such a height that we have to bear to the left, parallel with the hills. It is absolutely necessary that we should leave the Kizil-Aguin. We fail at our first attempt, but we go on a little further, and quit the bed and banks of the river after herculean efforts. It is five o'clock, and there is a piercing wind from the west. Our exertions have bathed us in sweat, and when I say "we," I include the horses. This nasty wind appears to be a speciality of the Pamir, and it is a sign that we are getting close to it.

We climb up and down the hills, following the ridges as much as possible. At 6.15 p.m., we halt in a hollow, where we find two saddled horses grazing, and we are much puzzled at their presence, which, however, inspirits us somewhat. Sadik and a Kirghiz take hold of these horses and mount them, giving us their own to hold while they go in search of the owners. They have discovered, by certain peculiar marks, that these horses do not belong to the Kara-Kirghiz of the Alaï. The find is an excellent one, just as we are entering upon the river of Kizil-Art, for these men will be of great help to us.

After our two scouts have been gone about twenty minutes, one of them comes galloping up and tells us that he has descried men and sheep in the direction of the river. As he is telling us this, Sadik arrives, driving two Kirghiz before him. They do not seem very well at ease, and make low bows, which express their sense of disquiet. They had seen us coming, and their first impulse had been to hide themselves. They did not show themselves until they saw strangers riding their horses. They invite us to their bivouac, which, they tell us, is in a "snug place,"

CHINESE KARA-KIRGHIZ.

and they show us the way to a ravine which is sheltered from the night wind, where a flock of sheep and goats is assembled. A thin column of smoke is curling up from a fire made of the droppings with which the soil is covered, and the Kirghiz heap it up and sleep on it, covered with arkar skins. This place is called Urtak.

The master of the shelter spreads out some skins for us and offers us a supper which consists of mutton boiled in water with a pronounced flavour of dung, either because the melted snow in which the mutton had been boiled contained some, or because the smoke from the fire had got into the coffee pot. For it is in a coffee-pot (*kumgane*) that these people cook their food. They have no other cooking vessel. They tear off pieces of meat with their fingers, and all drink the gravy in turns out of the coffee pot. There is no salt in it. While we are partaking of this delicious dish, our host tells us his story.

"I had gone to sell some sheep at Kashgar, where, I was told, they would fetch a good price, but I soon found the contrary. I bought a few others, and I retraced my steps by the Markan-Su. I was overtaken by the winter, and the snow began to fall. I had very great difficulty in crossing the Kizil-Art, where I lost two horses and all my baggage. I have halted here, where my sheep and goats can find a little of last year's grass still left. I had determined to await the return of fine weather with my servant, for we could not attempt to cross the Alaï and the Taldik. We have been living on our sheep and goats. We have not a grain of salt left, and this coffee pot is our sole cooking utensil, while we have very little flint left to light our fire with. But as there is abundance of dung, we keep it constantly alight so as not to be obliged to make a fresh fire every day. I don't know what would have become of us but for your arrival. If you will allow us, we will start to-morrow, following the path you have traced, and we shall reach the Ferghana. I have some acquaintances in the neighbourhood of Osch, for I am an Uzbeg from the banks of the Syr, and my servant is from Sarikol."

"When did you cross the Kizil-Art?"

"Several weeks ago."

"Do you think we shall be able to get across it?"

"I don't think so. The snow is very deep, and horses with loads on their backs will never get over it."

This is a bad piece of news, and after a harassing march of nine hours, we deserved a better fate. But the site is a good one, there are plenty of sheep, and enough grass to keep the fire going. We must take a day's rest and regale our men with mutton, resuming our march with renewed strength. As to the shepherd, he must not start until we do, so that we may get as much information as possible out of him. Our men will converse with him, and this will give them more pluck to go on. He does not seem to object to remaining, as he asks us when we shall allow him to start.

But our baggage does not arrive, and this is not surprising. We have no tent, and must sleep in the open air. My horse's quarters will make me an excellent pillow, and Menas, no doubt, has in his bag something to eat and some tea. Unfortunately, he has entrusted it to a Kirghiz who has not yet come in, and he has neither teapot, sugar, nor tea. This makes me very angry, for I have told him over and over again always to keep a day's provisions and enough tea to last several days on his person. But he is hopelessly careless in this respect.

We make the best of it all, and the wind howls over our heads with such fury that I determine to take refuge among the sheep and goats. A he-goat, whom I remark the next morning as having a very intelligent countenance, rests his head against mine, and I take care not to move. A ewe lies down at my feet, another licks the ice off my clothes and then lies full length upon me. A delicious sense of warmth pervades my body, and I go to sleep dreaming pleasantly. But my dreams do not last long, for I am awoke by part of the flock, which has been seized by one of those panics to which sheep are prone, passing over my body. It is in vain that I attempt to resume my place among them, for they have taken fright and make off when I come near them. My only resource is to crouch down before a low fire which just prevents me from freezing. My companions as well as myself endeavour to shake off the numbing sensation which comes over us. There are only about twelve degrees below zero, but the wind is incessant, and any one who has been upon an exposed place in winter, when a cold wind is blowing, knows what that is like. Upon the other hand, the stars seem to be larger and to show more light than they do in Europe.

March 20th.

At 6 a.m., the cold is almost as intense.

Pepin's face is terrible to look at, being all swollen, with his lips an enormous size, and blood oozing from the chaps. He cannot open his eyes or see a yard in front of him. Capus also has his face very much swollen, his nose is streaked like that of a leper, and his best friends would scarcely recognize him. It appears that I am not quite such an object, and this is because I have a thicker skin, according to Menas, who is also in a very sorry state.

We send to meet the pack-horses, which arrive about nine o'clock. The tent is put up, and the sun warms us a little. We

NIGHT TIME AT URTAK.

shall take a much needed rest to-day and to-morrow. Moreover, the owner of the flock sticks to his pessimist views, and according to him the Kizil-Art would be impassable, while as to passing by way of the Akbaital it is no use thinking about it. If we go by the Rang-Kul we risk meeting the Chinese outposts which would stop us. Sadik himself takes this view, and yet only yesterday he was very sanguine, though it is true that he then thought the Kizil-Art was open. To judge by the whiteness of the peaks which adjoin that pass it is not so.

All our Kirghiz men have their eyes affected; they complain of a bad headache and the horses are nearly done for. Four or five more such days, and there would be an end to the whole expedition. The first thing we have to do is to line our stomachs well. We purchase two sheep from the Uzbeg, and we give a treat to our men, infusing courage into them by way of their stomachs. The sun aids us, for at 2 p.m. we have ninety-five degrees and only seven degrees of frost in the shade. The day is a beautiful one and makes us forget the previous one. All our men are as active and brisk as a family of peasants when they kill a fatted pig. Abdur-Rasul, the poet, makes us a delicious sausage out of the liver, kidneys, and fat of the sheep, and we enjoy it exceedingly.

We grease our boots, dry our clothes, furbish up our arms, groom our horses, and repair the saddles and girths. The Kirghiz shave their heads, and we are glad to hear sounds of laughter and even singing. Rachmed cracks jokes which evidently amuse the Kirghiz, for they grin and show their teeth. He has got rid of his pelisse, and drawing in his belt he shows me that he is three inches thinner in less than six days. He looks quite unhappy at his shrinking figure, and deplores it in the most comical way imaginable.

The men who are ill from the cold rub their cheeks with tallow and bathe their eyes with warm water. Satti-Kul, the guide, is very lazy, but it is true that his eyes are much swollen, and he keeps his head down as if he was looking for something. But in reality, it is because he does not want to exert himself. When questioned as to the nature of the route we have before us, his invariable reply is "God alone can tell!"

Two men and two horses are missing, and we don't know what has become of them. We have twenty-two left.

As the sun goes down, so do our spirits. Before nightfall, we get the horses together, and they are attached by the feet with a long rope stretched along the ground and held down by iron

ENCAMPMENT FACING THE RAZED ARK

clamps; and the men collect around the fires lighted close to the baggage, and they converse for some time, seated upon their heels, with folded arms and the body bent forward to catch the warmth of the fire. Some of them, more fatigued than the rest, lie down at once and go to sleep, with their legs curled well up under them so as to be warmer. This is just what vagabonds in Europe do when they sleep in the open air.

In the group of which Sadik forms part, the conversation is being carried on in a low tone, and I send Menas to listen. He crawls along noiselessly, and gets within hearing without having

THE PLOT.

been heard or seen. When he comes back, he has a very interesting story to tell me.

The "master of the flock," Sadik and the principal men of our convoy were debating as to what course should be pursued. They were all agreed that the journey could not be continued, that it was madness to attempt to get through this snow, and that the best plan would be for us to retrace our steps. Before doing so, pits would be dug at this place, and all the barley and baggage we did not require buried in them, while we went to Gultcha, or Osch, to await the fine weather. In the month of July, we should return to the Alaï, and cross the Kizil-Art without any trouble. This was a very prudent plan, no doubt, and testified to the interest which these men took in us; but it did not suit our views. However, let us go to sleep now, and we can see what had best be done to-morrow.

March 21st.

We intend to rest all day again; but to-morrow we shall attempt to get over the Kizil-Art without a halt, at any cost. We had better leave the Kirghiz in the hope that we shall perhaps turn back. They spend the day in mending their equipment; and for their breakfast they eat the head, feet, and entrails of the sheep, cooked in an improvised oven excavated in the soil. No doubt they make an excellent meal.

Our encampment is very picturesque in the bright sunshine, and we look for all the world like a troop of brigands who have taken refuge, with their booty, in some safe spot, and are preparing for a fresh expedition. Our faces look as forbidding as you could wish.

SATTI-KUL.

To-day, the hideously ugly Satti-Kul is inclined to do a little work, and he splits some wood in very easy-going fashion, stopping now and then to suck a bone, which he then splits open with his hatchet in order to extract the marrow, grinning like some horrible gorilla.

SATTI-KUL HELPING TO COOK.

Then he comes up to the fire and looks to the coffee-pots, all of a row, which are filled with snow. I ought to have already explained by what a very simple process we obtain our water. The fire is lighted and the saucepan filled with snow, which is melted by the heat. The water is drawn off, when it congeals upon reaching freezing point, and it is put into a coffee-pot.

where it becomes water. This water is poured into another coffee-pot, where it becomes lukewarm; and then into a third, where it gets hot, and so into another, till it reaches the special kumgane in which boiling water is made for the tea. Satti-Kul is very fond of ladling out this hot water with a wooden spoon, but he does not like going to fetch clean snow in a bag.

Owing to the altitude—we are about 7800 feet above the level of the sea—the meat cooks badly, and the tea has not the flavour it possesses upon low ground. The water boils too quickly.

To-morrow will be a momentous day for us. We shall know if the gate of the Pamir is open or closed.

The night will be a fine one, with a clear sky and no wind. At 7 p.m., the thermometer is not much below zero.

Several of the horses are blind, that of Pepin among others, and so, too, is his owner. Menas remarks during the evening that some of our barley had been stolen. The Kirghiz must have given some to their horses, and thrown away more on the road, with the intention of picking it up as they return. They have also thrown away some wood. Once through the Kizil-Art, we will make them suffer for this.

March 22nd.

At 7 a.m., nearly forty degrees of frost, with a little wind from the east.

The shepherds are told they may go their way, and they are overjoyed. We have the horses loaded, and then we intimate to Sadik that we are starting for the Kizil-Art, that the other Kirghiz must help us to get through the pass, otherwise there will be some heads broken—his first of all. We are determined not to go back to Ak-Basoga before having ascertained that the Kizil-Art is impassable, and that the Pamir is not "fordable."

If this plateau resembles that of the Alaï, the enterprise is not more than we can manage. Sadik and the others listen in silence, without making a gesture or moving a muscle. A slight contraction of the eyelids is the only sign of emotion.

"Iakchi!" ("Very good!") says Sadik. And they all get up and make their horses ready.

Rachmed will bring up the rear, and, revolver in hand, will compel any one who attempts to turn back to go on. Menas will follow the first squad, and he has received similar orders. We ourselves start at once with Sadik and the three men whom the

THE ASCENT OF THE KIZIL-ART.

Kirghiz obey. The caravan gets into motion under our eyes, and then we take the lead, for we have to trace the route.

At the confluence of the Kizil-Aguin and Kizil-Art rivers, there are very deep drifts of snow, and at more than one place we have to climb on to the hills which skirt the banks. Below, we should be buried in over six feet of loose snow. At last we light upon a clear track, and we reach the Kizil-Art, feeling beneath our feet the ice upon its surface, the north-east wind having swept off all the snow.

ENCAMPMENT FACING THE KARA-KUL PASS.

So far the route is a good one; but as soon as we turn to the left, towards the pass, we find ourselves in a narrow defile, with enormous quantities of snow. It is, of course, impossible to follow the ordinary route along the thalweg, and so we pick out upon the sides of the valley the places where there is the least snow, sometimes on the right, sometimes on the left bank, and advance as best we can.

After six hours' marching—severe ascents and descents, interspersed with plenty of falls—we arrive at a spot where the valley becomes a gorge. We cannot yet see the summit of the pass, and men and horses alike are stretched out like so many dying forms upon a flat rock. We are bathed in sweat, and can scarcely open our eyes. We have violent headaches, and are parched with thirst, putting handfuls of snow into our mouths.

Sadik points with his finger to the white mass which bars the way, and with a motion of the head asks if we are to go on.

I look at the white masses of rock, which the sun is tinting with the rosy hues on a virgin's cheek, and virgin they are. "Aida, Sadik!" ("Forward!") Sadik puts his hand up to his beard, and turning towards Mecca, says—

"Bismallah! in the name of God!" in the tone of a man who is submitting to an inexorable fate. And off he starts, sounding the snow with his staff. Then he drops, picks himself up again, falls a second time and struggles in vain to extricate himself. However, we pull him out of the hole into which he has floundered, and as soon as he has recovered his breath, he sets off again. The three Kirghiz take the lead in turn, and every now and then one of them goes off to look for a passage. And one follows the other, puffing and blowing, and floundering about.

Above us we can see flocks of *arkars* (wild sheep), which gaze down upon us. Our presence surprises but does not apparently alarm them. We do not bestow so much as a chance shot upon them. Then we observe a heap of horns placed upon a *mazar* (tomb) which marks the summit of the thalweg. We cannot pass that way, so we bend to the left over the ridges and we descend upon the other side, on to the Pamir. After ten hours' march, at 6.15 p.m., we are encamped upon the dividing line, at an altitude of about fifteen thousand feet, with the valley of Markan-Su at our feet.

This is another day which those who have gone through it will never forget. We are all of us fatigued to death, but we are satisfied with the result, and the country seems a pleasant one, even to Rachmed, who would like it better, however, if it was more thickly populated, for he is fond of company. We experience

SADIK COOKING.

the satisfaction of those who have found what they have been seeking, and while the horses one after another are returning to the bivouac, to which they are attracted by showing them their *tourba* (wooden bowl) full of barley, I cast a glance at the south, in the direction of Lake Kara-Kul. Above the heights which surround the small plain of Markan-Su, which lies at our feet, is visible an immense gap, above which floats slowly in the sky a single cloud, round and white, like a snowball which has been hurled into the air, and which, having suddenly become deprived of its gravity, is arrested in its fall.

As far as the eye can reach, there is nothing to be seen but undulating mountains, with peaks rearing their heads aloft like proud sultans amid a prostrate crowd.

We made a copious meal of rice, millet, and meat, and having written out our diary by a candle which we have some difficulty in lighting, as it is frozen, we talk of home, and are quite cheerful.

If only it does not snow to-morrow! The plain looks well, and I am hopeful. But let us get some sleep, and leave to-morrow to take care of itself. We have scaled the last rampart which protects the "roof of the world."

STARTING FOR THE KARA-KUL.

CHAPTER XII.

THE PAMIR (*continued*).

At Lake Kara-Kul—Some of the men follow, the others are sent back—We remain eight in all—A track—A find—Satti-Kul as a nurse—Numberless wild sheep—The wind—Mount Kol—Tempest in the Kizil-Djek—Abandoned—The Rang-Kul; Kirghiz and Kutasses—Scenery—Negotiations—The mercury freezes—A polar night—Caprices of the temperature—Attempt to stop us—We are on Chinese territory—We do not wait for permission from Kashgar—All aid refused us—How we procure what we absolutely require.

March 23rd.

WHEN we awake, at 6 a.m., there are 15½ degrees below zero and no wind, at seven o'clock 11¼ degrees, and at half-past seven eight degrees.

The sun shines very brightly and warms us, the day being a magnificent one. The troop which comprises the barley-stealers is got together, and Rachmed, after duly reproaching them with their conduct, says that half of them will be sent back, but will not be given the certificate which they have to produce to their chiefs as evidence of good behaviour. The rest are to carry to the Kara-Kul the barley which remains, and this will relieve in some measure our horses, to which we shall not be able to give such large rations as we had intended doing when they were loaded. The men do not say anything, as they know that they are in the wrong and that resistance would be useless. Rachmed and Menas are to keep a sharp look-out on them. We descend into the valley with the hesitation of persons who get into the water without knowing its depth, and who are afraid of putting their feet into a hole.

We go forward, and as we advance we gradually gain assurance, for there is little more than two feet of loose snow, as fine as powdered sugar and not unlike the dust which one sees upon the road in summer time upon a frozen foundation. The faces of our men expand into a smile, and they sit their horses with more confidence. We arrive by a defile at a small lake which Sadik calls Kizil-Kul. It is thawing at the surface, and there is a thin stream of water which is scarcely salt at all and of which we drink several stoops with great gusto. All around us are hills still white with snow, with the sand visible on some of the lower slopes, and flocks of *arkars* (wild sheep) skipping about on them. The leaders of the flock see us and halt upon the summit, looking at us with a good deal of suspicion. The rams, with their drooping dewlaps and long twisted horns, are noble-looking animals. A shot fired at them sends them flying, and they scale the steepest slopes at a wonderful pace. At each turn, we come upon flocks of these fine animals, feeding in groups of ten, fifteen, or twenty, and scraping up the snow with their feet to get at the roots. We emerge from the region of Kizil-Kul, which is so undulating that one would never fancy one was in a mountainous country.

Beyond Kizil-Kul, the snow is again rather deep, being up to the horses' chests. We have several falls while traversing the *davan* (pass) which leads to the basin of Lake Kara-Kul. From the top of the pass, we can descry a corner of the lake, at the extremity of the valley, through which the river of Guk-Seï flows when the snow melts. We pass by blocks of rock amid which several hares are scuttling off, just to remind us that we are upon the Pamir-Kargoch (Pamir of the hares). Gradually we get in

THE KARA-KUL, AS SEEN FROM THE PASS.

sight of the whole lake, the surface of which glitters with ice, while it is shut in by snow-clad mountains.

The north-east of the lake is skirted by a plain about a mile broad. We can see something moving upon the surface of the lake and wonder whether it can be a flock or herd. Sadik and Satti-Kul assert that they are sheep, and that further on they can see some *oui* (felt tents). They ask to be allowed to go on in advance and ascertain whether this is so. The prospect of coming upon tents puts us all in a good humour, for there are no tents without men being with them, and if there are men, we shall find flocks, milk, beasts of burden, and helpers. Moreover, man is a sociable being, and we shall be glad of a little company.

At last we get close to the level of the lake, and what we took for a rather flat plain is dotted with hillocks and intersected by the sandy beds of streams, which are at present dry.

Sadik identified just now the course of the Kara-Art. There are footprints upon the sand, and we can tell that arkars and hares have been by here during the day; while further on there are traces of birds hopping about, and of rodents having nibbled at the roots. But most of these marks are not recent, and the place must be the site of a *laïlag* (temporary summer encampment) of the Kara-Kirghiz. We have been marching for eight hours and a half, and it being now 6.30 p.m., it is time to encamp.

We look out for some creek at the edge of the lake, where we shall be protected from the wind. I go forward in search of a good bivouac, and find one which will suit us. Just then I catch sight of a flock of arkars, and they see me; so while I gallop forward to try and cut them off, they scuttle off in the direction of the mountain. It is no use trying to overtake them, though a fat arkar would, no doubt, be a very toothsome morsel, besides giving us a change of diet. To appease our great hunger, we munch some wheaten cakes, which are so hard that they have to be broken with a hammer. Our baggage and cooking utensils have not yet arrived, so I don't know at what time we shall get our supper. Sadik and his companion return without having been able to see anything of flocks or tents, and they have been the victims of a not uncommon delusion. At nine o'clock the baggage horses arrive at the bivouac, to which they have been guided by the fire we have made with the droppings collected round the encampment. At 11.30 p.m., "supper is on the table," and we eat our boiled mutton and rice with a hearty appetite, despite our being at an altitude of 12,800 feet.

March 24th.

At 8 a.m., there are thirty-six degrees of frost.

The Kirghiz who had stolen the barley are missing, and they must have turned back before reaching the pass which leads to the lake. Several sacks of barley are missing; and as we suppose that they must have been thrown down into the snow, we send Rachmed, two Kirghiz, and the horses which are the least fatigued, to gather up all the fragments.

The Kirghiz of Mollah-Baïas, who have served us well, will be sent back this evening with a handsome *douceur* apiece, after we have treated them to a good meal. We employ them all day to pick up the droppings of the stock, and to dig up roots for our fire, and they get several bags full. Satti-Kul has told us that we shall find nothing of the kind further on; and he calls these roots "kiskenne."

We have a good encampment, and it is quite warm in the sun, which is not reflected by the snow, the wind having fortunately cleared it away. At noon, there are only six degrees of frost in the shade, while in the sun the thermometer marks fifty.

We take advantage of this exceptional temperature to "clean ourselves" a little. Our horses have been put out to feed, and they have taken possession of the pasturages vacated by the arkars, not one of which is visible in the plain.

At three o'clock, our men return with four sacks of barley; and after careful calculation we find that we have enough left to last us ten days. We must go by the Rang-Kul, where we are certain to find beasts of burden. But instead of avoiding inhabited places, we shall endeavour to find them. We must, at any cost, relieve our horses, and only utilize them at the last extremity. This will create a good deal of difficulty, but we shall get out of it somehow.

In the afternoon, we remark flocks of larks and starlings flying

ENCAMPMENT UPON THE KARA-KUL.

in the direction of the wind (south-west). They alight, but soon rise again. We receive a visit from a chaffinch, which is either very confiding or very hungry, for he comes to look for a few crumbs at the entrance to our tent. We receive him with great cordiality, and, for an hour or more he amuses us by the way in which he hops about, half at his ease, half afraid; but as soon as he has satisfied his appetite, he flies off with an impudent twitter.

A number of birds fly over our heads at a great height, uttering cries which we cannot at all recognize. We ask Satti-Kul what they are, and all the answer we can get is that they are "birds" (*dourmas*). Sadik explains to us that they are birds which have the plumage of a duck, and the head of a cormorant. They are not to be found in the plain of the Ferghana, and like cold countries. During the summer, they frequent the pools of the Pamir. He adds, that when they are fat they make very good eating.

Thereupon, the chief of the Kirghiz who are remaining with us, and with whom we are very well satisfied, asks us if we will give him a *kaghaz* (paper), as he wants to take advantage of the fine weather and start at once. He is afraid that a snowstorm may block the path to the Alaï, and that he and his men will be unable to get through.

We hand him the certificate which testifies to his good service, with a short letter for our host and friend, General Karalkoff. We distribute some presents to these brave fellows; and Baïch, their young leader, who had gone on his knees like the others, gets up and, stooping forward, puts his hand to his beard. The others do the same, and exclaim, "Amin! amin! Allah Akbar."

We shake hands with them, Kirghiz fashion, and off they start, soon disappearing out of our sight. Their departure makes a deep impression upon our troop, and the sudden silence shows that those who remain behind are heavy at heart. We are now only eight in all, and there is still a long way to go, and many risks to encounter. As long as there was a large number of men, there was not the feeling of isolation which now supervenes and makes them look so gloomy. Rachmed, who is fond of company, is the most sombre of all. I remark that he remains for a few moments motionless, watching the last glimmer of sunlight, and pulling the hairs out of his beard and biting them with his teeth, which is with him an unmistakable sign of his being pre-occupied. Then he goes to the bag in which the bread is kept, breaks off a bit and munches it, picks up the nosebags of the horses and gives them some barley, singing at the top of his voice as if to drive away dull care.

After supper, Rachmed, who no doubt is anxious to divert his thoughts into another channel, relates to his listening companions the story of "the merchant's son," to the great dismay of Abdur-Rasul, and to the great delight of Sadik, who listens open-mouthed and with sparkling eyes. Menas, who, as usual, is in fits of laughter when his friend draws the long-bow, eventually begins to snooze; while Satti-Kul is fast asleep, with his legs crossed and his head in his chest. He has eaten too much millet.

March 25th.

At 5 a.m., there are eighteen degrees below zero.

At 7.15 a.m., we prepare for a start, the thermometer marking eleven below zero, and about forty degrees in the sun.

We intend to encamp to the south-east of the Kara-Kul, where the horses will find a little grass. Our men have great difficulty in dividing the iouks and loading them. The bales have to be made according to the strength of the horses, and well balanced, which is not to be done in moment. It is only upon the march that any error which may have been made can be detected; and as Rachmed is the only one who, thanks to a lengthy experience, is really clever at doing this—a package is continually falling off or a saddle turning round, so that we have to be constantly stopping to put things straight. We advance but slowly, and the stoppages are so frequent that Menas will have it that the devil has something to do with it.

Some birds settle down near to us, and, owing to the undulation of the ground, I get a shot at them and kill three. They are lagopedes, with an orange-coloured head and ash-coloured backs. We shall have them roasted for this evening.

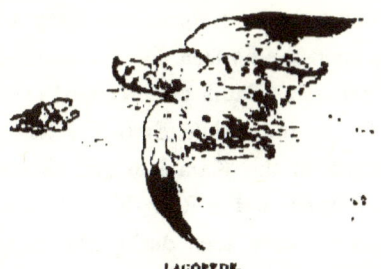

LAGOPEDE.

But the guide, Satti-Kul, whom I have overtaken, stops his horse, and pointing to marks in the snow, says that they are recent. As a matter of fact, the wind has not had time to blow back the blades of grass which emerge from the snow. The footsteps are in the direction of the lake, coming from the mountain. After we have established our encampment, we will try and discover the "leather stocking" who has made these footprints.

We pass a number of small pools which are the frozen lagoons of the Kara-Kul. Close to the lake there are hills composed of a sort of peat, which Satti-Kul calls "pachta-kattin," and which he says that we shall use for our fire to-night. There are some hills which glitter like large glass balls, with a coat of slippery ice from which trickle small rivulets of water more or less salt. These rivulets trickle over the ice and disappear as soon as the sun has gone down, freezing before one's very eyes, so to speak.

We fix our bivouac at the extreme south-east end of the lake, upon the sand, close to the peat. We go to have a look at the Kara-Kul, and find that it would bear thousands of guns, and that millions of skaters could assemble upon it without the least danger.

Pepin tries to make a water-colour drawing of a lagopede, but he has to give it up; although he uses hot water, the paper gets crusted with ice wherever it is shaded by his hand.

We tether our horses and keep a sharp look-out on them; as also upon the horizon, for the footprints we have seen keep us on the *qui-vive*. Sadik goes forward to reconnoitre.

In the meanwhile, Satti-Kul tells us that he has spent eight summers at the Kara-Kul, and that one of his sisters is married to a Kirghiz of the Rang-Kul. I ask him what he thinks of the tracks we have seen during the day, and what this man can be doing here. He will not say more than " I don't know."

As the sun goes down, we see Sadik coming towards us, and close beside him a large object which has not the outline of a man on horseback. We all strain our eyes to see what it can be, and Abdur-Rasul, who has very good sight, says that it is a camel. So it proves to be; but what, we ask one another, can it be that he has got slung across the saddle. All we can tell is that it is not a sheep. At last we see that he is leading a she camel with a piece of rope, and that what he is carrying is her offspring, only a few days old. Satti-Kul takes it into his arms and at once constitutes himself its nurse. The little camel begins to bleat, and we all laugh very much.

Rachmed declares that Providence has sent us this camel to carry our baggage.

Sadik reports to us the result of his search. He followed the footsteps, which put him on the fresh track of the camels, and as he thought that the camel would be easier to catch than the man, especially as the mother would not abandon her young, he went after it. So he brought it back, believing that its owner will come in to claim it, and that we shall be able to obtain some service from him in exchange. So we shall have to sleep with one eye open to-night. No doubt he has gone to tell some of his friends, who are hidden in the gorge. He must have seen Sadik and got out of his way.

The lagopedes are delicious, eaten with mutton and roasted in the pan.

The temperature varies very much, for at 7.15 a.m. the thermometer was eleven degrees below zero in the shade, while in the sun it was about thirty-eight degrees. At 7.40 a.m., it was eight

SADIK'S CAPTURE.

degrees below zero, and thirty-eight; at 8 a.m., it was five below zero, and fifty-five; at 9 a.m., there were twenty-seven degrees of frost in the shade, while in the sun the thermometer was at seventy-two.

About 3 p.m., a breeze sprang up from the south-west, and there are eighteen degrees of frost in the shade, while in the sun the thermometer is at forty-eight. At 4 p.m., the thermometer is nearly at zero; while at 8.40 p.m., there are only fourteen degrees of frost, so we keep well wrapped up to guard against these sudden changes.

March 26th.

At 5.20 a.m., the thermometer is just below zero.

During the night, the horses have been put out to graze in the marshy fields, carefully watched by the men, while the new-born camel, well wrapped up in felt, has passed the night at his mother's side. Now that the sun has come out, he has been uncovered, and he evidently enjoys it, wagging his almost invisible little tail with pleasure. With his head down, and his legs bent under his stomach, he looks something like a seal sunning itself. The mother looks at him tenderly, and then raises her head, as if proud of having brought so splendid an animal into the world. She gets on to her feet, and opens her legs in order that her little one may, with the help of Satti-Kul, get at her udder and suck to the full.

The horses are loaded, and we start with them, and we do not intend to take the camel with us, nor even to eat the young camel, as Rachmed, who would, I believe, devour human flesh, proposed that we should. We have given the subject great consideration, but have finally rallied to the opinion of Sadik, who thinks that we ought not to make enemies if we can possibly avoid it. The Kirghiz would regard the use of the camel as a robbery, and they would take their revenge for it if possible. Sadik says that he and Abdur-Rasul would certainly be made to suffer for it on their way back.

We soon saw that he was right, for we had scarcely raised the camp, when two mounted Kirghiz, followed by dogs, came to fetch the stray camel, and recognized Abdur-Rasul.

We pass over a red and stony steppe, with very little snow. As we get further away from the Kara-Kul, which is so soon no more than a thin white streak, the plain closes in like a gulf, and we shall get out of it through a narrow gap which we can just discern in the mountain. This desert region is dotted here and there with large drifts of snow, upon which numerous flocks of arkars may be seen standing. They have got their heads down into the snow, seeing what they can grub out; but one of them stands sentinel. He sees us coming and gives the alarm, and the whole flock, after standing still for a moment to look at us, is off to the mountain.

These patches of snow and the arkars do not extend beyond the plain of Kara-Kul. The east wind blows with great violence off the bare mountain chain, and freezes us to the marrow. Upon reaching the mazar of Ak-Salir, a very ancient saint according to Sadik, upon whose tomb are piled an endless number of horns, we reach the confluence of several open valleys. We do not select that of Mus-Kul, but we mount towards the north-east, and making the circuit of an arid ridge of rocks, we arrive by a fairly good road at the lake of Mus-Kul (Lake of Ice), so-called, according to Satti-Kul, because it never thaws. The level of the lake is very high, and the summer path lies hidden beneath the ice. So we are obliged to climb higher, to the slope of some hills, which do not form a very convenient bivouac. We encamp at the broadest part of the valley, to the south of that of Ak-Baïtal, upon the edge of the ice which surrounds the meadows where we put our horses to graze. We cannot contrive to shelter ourselves from the wind, which has been the means of clearing away all the snow here, whereas the passes of Kizil-Djek and of Ak-Baïtal, the approaches to which we can descry, are white with snow, as well as the heights overlooking them.

The Kizil-Djek is clear, but the neighbouring Ak-Baïtal is gloomy, and a snowstorm, descending from it, gathers additional force on the way, and very nearly suffocates us. The wind hampers our breathing, and the descending storm seems as if about to crush us, but the wind suddenly veers round, a strong gust bursts in upon us from the north-west, and descends like a cold douche upon our shoulders, clearing the valley and routing the tempest from the Ak-Baïtal. Not that we are much better off, for we are all of us shivering, and feel half suffocated. About 6 p.m., the wind shifts, and goes round again to the east, blowing more fiercely than ever.

Eating our supper as quickly as possible, and huddling ourselves beneath our sheepskin, we sleep, thanks to our seven hours' march, despite the howlings of the tempest. Every now and

KIZIL-DJEK.

then we are awakened by a choking sensation, which compels us to raise ourselves for an instant to a sitting posture.

March 27th.

At 6.30 a.m., the thermometer marks about twenty-three degrees of frost, and it is lucky there is no more, for with this east wind, we might not be able to proceed if the cold was more severe.

We make a start at nine, marching eastward. We are obliged to march over ice, which forms the flooring of a narrow passage, along which a tremendous draught is blowing. Our horses, which step very cautiously, cannot help falling, however, and it is rather difficult to load them again, for they are very unsteady on their legs. We march for more than an hour over this ice, ascending all the time till we reach some cliffs, and at each step we come upon snow-drifts in the hollow places and along the sides of the rock, with arkar horns and salt lying on the grass. In many places we see dried-up watercourses, with sandy beds. The valley gradually opens out, and about noon the snow begins again, covering everything with its mantle of white. Valleys and gorges extend right and left of us, and facing us we see the saddle-backed pass of Kizil-Djek. We keep climbing up amid the pitiless wind and snow, with occasional falls, and halting every now and then to get breath.

At three o'clock, we reach the summit of the pass, about 15,700 feet, and the wind, incensed no doubt at our presumption, redoubles its efforts, and, as Rachmed says, brings one's heart into one's mouth. We are literally suffocating, and there is a noise in our ears as if a million *bayadères* were drumming into them with their tambourines. And then this abominable wind—which takes us for dead, no doubt, in which it is mistaken—envelops us in whirlwinds of snow as in a winding-sheet, and drives handfuls of it in our faces, just as a grave-digger hastily buries the dead the night after the battle. But this is a battle we intend to win. We take advantage of a slight lull to descend some very steep ridges as far as Uzun-Djilga, where we halt after a tramp of seven hours and fifty minutes which at times was little short of a funeral march. Our horses have their heads down almost to the ground, and it is the gamest which suffer the most, for, as a French general once said of his men, "it is always the same men who get themselves killed."

The snowstorm continues, and our alarms are not appeased until Rachmed and Abdur-Rasul make their appearance amid the thick flakes. We were afraid that they might pass clean by without seeing us.

Abdur-Rasul has a violent headache, but he has bled from the nose, and this has relieved him. All the men complain of severe pains on the chest. Poor old Sadik lies down without waiting for his supper, the millet porridge of which he is so fond, and which will not be ready just yet, for it has taken half an hour to light a fire in a hole dug in the ground, the soil being frozen as hard as the meat, which is like a piece of wood.

We go to sleep amid the howling of the tempest. Now and then we are awakened by a suffocating feeling, but we gradually get used to it, for we generally have a heavy sensation in the head. Looking through the aperture of the tent, I can see that the snow is still falling. Man, isolated and lost to sight amid this majestic disorder of nature, is lucky in being so small, for he is thus better able to elude its destructive action, and, like an insect, he is tenacious of life.

March 28th

The morning opens unfavourably. The men complain, when they awake, that they suffer very much in the head, and that they were cold all night. They are dispirited and devoid of all energy; but I am obliged to tell them to prepare some tea and light the fire. At seven o'clock, there are still thirty degrees of frost, with a westerly wind, a cloudy sky, and a few flakes still falling. We must wait till the sun comes out, as that will cheer them up, and our stage to-day must be only a short one.

The horses have not much vigour left, for they are all bleeding from the nose, and do not attempt to snort. Two or three of them stand with their backs to the wind, and another of them will not advance to have the nosebag thrown over his neck, though he can hear the barley being shaken up in it. This is a

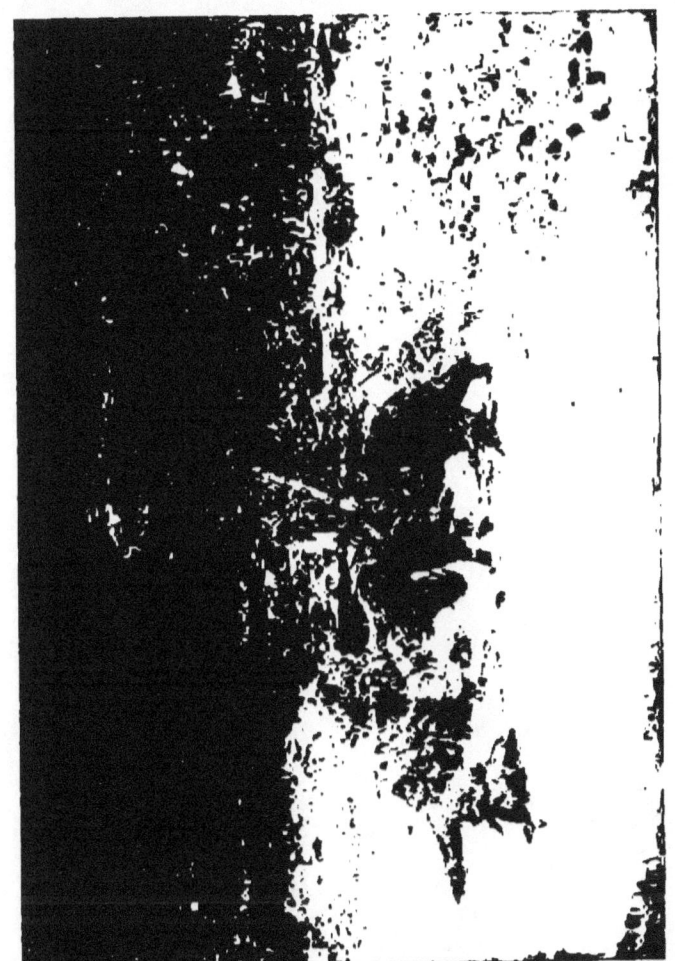

IN THE PASS OF KIZIL-DZEK.

bad sign, and he, like one or two of the others, will never get the whole stage.

The preparations for a start are made without the usual interchange of jokes, and as the sun does not deign to show himself, we start with a west wind blowing at our backs. Having come down from the plateau upon which we had encamped into the valley which winds away eastward, we are once more in the trackless snow. Satti-Kul goes on in front, and as he is suffering a good deal with his eyes, he leads us into some very queer places, so Sadik takes his place and acquits himself much better.

To the east-south-east, which is about the course we are taking, we can make out a white peak which we assume to be the Tagharma (Moustagata), the highest peak in the Pamir. It is thanks to the wind, which for a moment or so clears away the mist, that we are able to see it. But this bitter, cutting wind makes our march a very gloomy one, and not a word is exchanged.

A HORSE ABANDONED TO HIS FATE.

The horse which had suffered the most was not loaded, but he had followed us a little way, with drooping head and ears; but at length he stops, unable to go any further. We thought that he would go to Rang-Kul, where there is grass, it appears, and where he might have lived till the fine weather returned, and have regained strength. But he is fairly worn out, and lets his companions all go by in front. His poor legs cannot carry him any further; they are stiff from exposure, exhaustion, and cold, and he neighs feebly as we abandon him, just as a man at sea is abandoned when one cannot throw a life-belt to him, and whose death, certain though it be, one cannot well hasten. The poor brute is soon no more than a black speck, far in our rear, upon the white sheet of snow which will soon envelop him in its folds, when he sinks exhausted to the ground.

We go single file through the valley, which narrows and then opens again, where several gorges branch out to the left. All is rigid and white, with horns of dead arkars protruding here and there, while a number of live arkars appear in the distance, too wild to let us get near them, and flitting about like phantoms in a cemetery. There is no motion save that of the fine snow driven before the tempestuous wind. Snow, nothing but snow; no vegetation, not enough wood to make a match with. Our only distraction is when a horse falls, or loses his load, or steps out of the path; but at last, after five and a half hours' march, we reach the valley of Ichki, in the basin of the Rang-Kul, and we make for the south-east.

At a place called Kamara-Tag by Satti-Kul, who spent his childhood in this region, we take shelter in a grotto at the foot of an overhanging rock; and we are at the extreme end of a valley which descends in a straight line from the north—a perfect desert, as may well be imagined, and quite white.

While we are settling into our encampment upon the droppings accumulated by the flocks which have come to this natural shelter, we see to the right an eagle, which has scarcely the strength to fly; and to our left an emaciated crow, which perches above us and begins to croak. Like people who have been for a long time condemned to silence, he is very anxious to enter into conversation with some one; but he can scarcely emit a sound from his throat, which is hoarse from hunger.

Satti-Kul is delighted to see the land of his forefathers, who bear the name of the tribe of Ichk, borrowed from this valley, and he vaunts the charms of this grotto. It is the first shelter we have come across for a fortnight, and it will perhaps be the last until we have reached the other slope of the "roof of the world."

Satti-Kul smiles, and he is in a very good humour, for he points in the direction of Rang-Kul and says that it is quite close. Thereupon, he begins to fill the lappets of his pelisse with drop-

ENCAMPMENT AT KAMARA-TAG, BEFORE REACHING THE RANG-KUL.

pings, and endeavours to get near the saucepan, of which Sadik has the management as senior. But Sadik pushes him off, and mumbles something about not liking lazy fellows.

March 29th.

We treat ourselves to an hour or two's extra rest this morning, as the Rang-Kul is near, and we count upon finding there tents and some one to lend us a hand. At eight o'clock, there are twenty-five degrees of frost, but there is no wind, a cloudy sky, and a delicious temperature.

At ten o'clock, the mist clears away and the sun comes out, imparting a little courage to our men, who have been slowly loading the horses. When the sun disappears we are melancholy, but we do not suffer from the radiation and heat; but when he reappears we forget the pleasure he has given us, and mutter imprecations upon his dazzling force. People are never content with what they have got.

After two and a half hours' march, we reach the entrance to the basin of the Rang-Kul, with the valley of Ak-Baïtal, shrouded in white, to our right. We do not see the lake, which is hidden in a depression of the ground and covered with ice. But in summer, according to Satti-Kul, its level rises, and its waters cover a considerable part of the plain.

We keep our eyes open; and Satti-Kul, who has been scanning the horizon, exclaims, " Koutasse ; it is good !"

Koutasse means yak, and where there are yaks there are also men. This is not a bad piece of news, for the *morale* of our little troop wants being worked up; and we shall all be glad to see fresh faces. Our horses can hardly get along; and mine, which has done a great deal of work in the Alaï, is quite *hors de combat*. But we shall rest at Rang-Kul, and we shall ease our horses, thanks to the yaks which Satti-Kul has just seen, and to the camels which we encounter. It is true that they do not appear to be very flourishing, for their humps, protruding from a felt covering, are small and thin.

We pick our way amid ruts, past pools, on the banks of which are reed-beds, like those adjoining the lake of Kara-Kul. And after two hours' march we halt in the middle of the plain, a few hundred yards from the glaciers of the Rang-Kul. Arkar horns, droppings, and congealed footprints, some quite fresh, tell us that this place is frequented in summer by numerous flocks, and that even now a few are wandering about and finding a meagre pittance among the roots, with which we hope presently to make a good fire.

I measure several horns which are over four feet four inches long.

No one comes near our tent, though there must be several arkars prowling about in the neighbourhood, but they keep themselves in hiding until they are sure who we are. To-morrow we must send Sadik and Satti-Kul in search of a guide who can show us the road to Kunjut, of beasts of burden for the baggage, and, above all, of a sheep or a goat. It is pleasant occasionally to make a meal off an animal one has seen killed.

The sun is with us all day; but at 7.30 p.m. the thermometer marks thirty-one degrees of frost, while an hour or two later the sky clouds over, with a westerly breeze, and there are not more than twenty-three degrees. We must be prepared for snow.

March 30th.

It has snowed during the night. Sadik and Satti-Kul go, as soon as they are awake, in search of the owners of the animals which are wandering along the shores of the lake. They will try and find some one who has been to Kunjut recently, and who is able to give us some information. We don't know anything about this country which Satti-Kul tells us that we shall reach in ten days; whether it is independent, or whether it is subject to the Chinese, the people of Kashmir, the English, or the Afghans. The question is whether we can get there without passing by Ak-Tach, where we expect to have difficulties with the Chinese authorities. That is the point we have to ascertain. We should like, also, to avoid the province of Wakhan, where the Afghans have posts which would turn us back.

Yesterday, Sadik thought that we had better make for Tagharma, where we should find an abundance of everything, and whence we should easily get to the Kunjut by the Tag-Dumbach-Pamir in a week. But we should be in an inhabited region, and the beg might possibly assemble a force large enough to capture us without any chance of our resisting. He would send us to Kashgar, and there would be an end of our expedition.

The situation is a rather puzzling one. We are eager for our scouts to come back and bring with them some native of the Rang-Kul, who will tell us what is best to be done.

We are at an altitude of about 12,750 feet, the wind has gone

ENCAMPMENT UPON THE RANG-KUL, FACING THE TAGHARMA.

down, and we are able to breathe more freely than we have done for the last few days. Roots and dung abound, so we can boil plenty of water, having first melted the snow, and wash to our heart's content, which is all the more necessary that we have not had a chance of doing so for a fortnight. I say nothing about the vermin, for they are the least of our troubles. Let me speak rather of the view.

We see that the mountains form a circle around the steppes, and, as Rachmed observes, there is no visible outlet. To the south-east, opposite our tent, are jagged rocks of quartz, streaked with snow. Eastward are snowy mountains, with others behind them, and in another direction an arm of the Rang-Kul, to the right of which the Mustagata rears its lofty head to the sky. Behind us the mountains are seen dimly through the mist, while to the west are gigantic cones, upon the summit of which float clouds resembling smoke issuing from volcanoes. When the sun goes down, it lights up this wild scene and lends it an air of tenderness which seemed incompatible with such savage grandeur.

COUTASSES (YAKS).

In an easterly direction, we descry two black spots on the steppe, and these prove to be our two men returning, and none too soon, for night is falling fast.

Abdur-Rasul has been examining the yaks which I had been looking at in the morning and which had made a very favourable impression upon me. They are like large, lazy oxen, but as square and sturdy as a hippopotamus, with long hair trailing almost to the ground and a bushy tail like that of a horse. There is little intelligence in their eye, and they are constantly feeding and ruminating, their rapid digestion showing that they are cattle and not horses. They make a sort of grunting sound, but they seem very strong on their legs.

According to Abdur-Rasul, the flesh of the yak is good, better than that of the cow, and its milk is very nutritive. It can carry a heavier load than a pack-horse and can go a greater pace, but it must be well fed. In hot weather, the yak is useless. It is very vicious too, and those which are used for work always have the ends of their horns sawn off. He adds that they are very stupid animals.

"Do you think these can be of any use to us?" we ask him.

"I don't think so. They have scarcely anything to eat, and they are very weakly."

"Then they can never be of any use; in summer on account of the heat, in the winter because they are short of food."

"You are quite right. They make bad beasts of burden, but as they stand cold well in severe weather, when all other animals die, the Kirghiz is very glad to have them to keep him from starvation."

In fine, the yak might be employed in this country as a sort of living preserved meat which does not need tinning.

Abdur-Rasul arrives at the conclusion that we shall do best to make use of horses or camels, and he adds that the Pamir horses are very small.

While we are talking, the two men whom we had seen in the distance come up, and one of them has some one in the saddle behind him.

The new-comer gets off without saying a word, shakes hands with Abdur-Rasul, and then goes to kneel down by himself, away from the fire. He is a small man with a large Mongol face, much flatter than that of our Kirghiz. The nose is flat and the eyes so sunk as to be almost invisible, while the hands and feet are very short. He is an unmistakable Chinaman.

I ask Sadik who he is, and he answers, "Djuma-Bi," with something like a wink of the eye; a man who has had to leave the Alaï country, and because of some difficulty he has got into.

I ask him to draw up to our men's fire, and get him into conversation. He speaks in very unfavourable terms about the route, saying that all the passes, whether by the Ak-Baïtal or the Ak-Su are closed.

There is a great deal of snow, both this side and the other side of Ak-Tach, where we shall encounter Teïts, of the same blood as Satti-Kul, who, by the way, has, I think, washed his face. Neither he nor Sadik put in a word, and I suspect them of having schooled Djuma-Bi how to answer my questions. They do not say a word about the Karauls who have been posted by the Chinese.

DJUMA-BI.

Djuma-Bi knows the route very well, and the tracings which he makes on the ground with a piece of wood are quite correct.

He says, "On getting near to the Kunjut, we shall come upon some Karauls; they will go and tell the Kunjutis, who will come to meet us and bar the way."

"But you say that it is impossible to pass by way of the Ak-Baïtal or the Ak-Su?"

"That is why I think you should wait a fortnight here for fine weather."

"Then you know no other route except by the Ak-Baïtal or the Ak-Su?"

"No."

"You will be able to get us camels, or yaks, or horses?"

"Not now, they could not get along; in a fortnight they will be strong, and you will be able to start."

"We would only use them for one stage, and that would not tire them. We will pay you with *iambas* (bars of silver) which bear the Kashgar stamp."

Djuma-Bi does not make any answer.

"And how about the Kunjutis?" we ask him. "To whom do they pay tribute—to the Chinese or to the Kashgari?"

"I don't know at all. They are our enemies. Two years ago, they sought to make war upon us. But we had a great many yaks; and when they saw these animals, they thought that we were very numerous, and they were afraid to attack us. Our tribe had many yaks, but we lost nearly all our stock this last moon. We are poor."

But it is quite dark. To-morrow we shall know more. It is strange that no one alludes to a Chinese post, which must be somewhere near to where we are.

The cold will be terrific, for the thermometer, which at 7.10 p.m. marked thirty degrees of frost, stood at 8 p.m. at six degrees below zero, and at 8.30 p.m. at eight degrees below zero; at 9.45 p.m. the record is eighteen degrees below zero.

Our men cannot make up their minds to come away from the fire, and amuse one another with relating stories. The night is extraordinarily clear, and there is the most perfect calm in the atmosphere. The stars are very brilliant indeed, and our weak eyes can scarcely stand the unprecedented brightness of the crescent moon, which illuminates a cupola even more arrayed in gold than that of the Tillah Kari mosque at Samarcand.

I never saw the celestial vault loom so large as it did upon the Pamir, for the mountains seemed no more than slight elevations upon the surface of the earth, while the men grouped around our large fire, itself no more than a rushlight, looked like so many pigmies.

At 2.20 a.m., with the moon still so luminous that I could distinguish objects inside the tent, I go out to look at the thermometer, and find that the mercury has vanished. It has evidently been frozen. Thinking that I may be mistaken, I show the instrument to Capus; and we light a candle, the result being that we find the mercury really has frozen up, and is no bigger than a leaden pellet.

March 31st.

We never slept so soundly; and our sleep might be compared to the lethargy of an Alpine marmot. We cannot make up our minds to move, and it is ten o'clock when we get out from among our wraps.

At 10 a.m., there are fifty-five degrees in the sun, and four degrees below zero in the shade.

The following table, moreover, will show how capricious the climate of the Pamir is :—

Hour.	In the Shade.	In the Sun.
10.15 a.m.	2 degrees below zero	61 degrees.
10.30 ,,	½ ,, ,,	60 ,,
10.45 ,,	½ degree above zero	62 ,,
11.15 ,,	4 ,, ,,	68 ,,
11.25 ,,	4 ,, ,,	63 ,,
11.30 ,,	3 ,, ,,	50 ,,
1.0 p.m.	11 ,, ,,	46 ,,
4.30 ,,	26 ,, ,,	35 ,,
5.15 ,,	30 ,, ,,	36 ,,
6.20 ,,	21 ,, ,,	
6.35 ,,	14 ,, ,,	
8.45 ,,	5 ,, ,,	
9.0 ,,	4 ,, ,,	

During the night, Djuma-Bi has had a long conversation with Satti-Kul, who has given him all the news from the Alaï, while the former has told him about things in the Pamir. They had not met for a long time, both being of the Ichki family, and of the tribe of Teïts. Djuma-Bi has drunk large quantities of tea, and partaken freely of millet porridge. Perhaps he may be inclined to help us, and I sound him on the subject.

"Have you got any camels or yaks?"

"Yes."

"Will you let them to us?"

"Yes."

KIRGHIZ OF THE RANG-KUL.

"How much a day for each?"

"The fact is they are a long way off, and it would take a week to fetch them. I have only got sheep handy."

"Sell us some sheep."

"I can sell you one."

"Go and fetch it, and bring us at the same time some Kirghiz who will let us have camels."

"Camels are the best in the snow, because their legs are longer."

Djuma-Bi and Satti-Kul were about to start, when we saw what looked like three horsemen riding up, but they turned out to be men on foot, whose figures had been magnified by the mirage.

The nearer they get, the smaller they appear, and Pepin thought that they must be lads. But it turned out that two were full-grown men, one somewhat advanced in years, and the third a young man of twenty. All of them were nearly beardless, very wizened and undersized, with a few stray hairs falling from their upper lip by way of apology for a moustache. We receive them very politely, and press them to take plenty of tea and porridge. In answer to our inquiries, one of them asserts that we can pass by the Ak-Su, and that we shall find some Kirghiz there.

He will let us have three camels and a horse, but only as far as Kizil-Djilgua, because his animals have grown weak from their winter fast.

They are very amiable and ready with their offer of services. What can it all mean? for Djuma-Bi declared that we could not get over the Ak-Su.

At this moment other Kirghiz arrive, one of them riding a native Pamir horse no bigger than a donkey, and just the size for such diminutive riders.

They remain till nightfall beside our fire, the younger ones bringing roots and kisiak in bags to make it burn better. They will be able to keep warm all night, and we shall have a provision which will last us several days. We leave the Rang-Kul to-morrow, and shall have plenty more snow further on. Rachmed is still amusing the men with his stories when I go off to sleep.

April 1st.

We sleep like tops, and I believe that if we did not struggle to shake off this torpor, we should await fine weather at the Rang-Kul rolled up in our sheepskins.

Fortunately we have a clear object in view, and I bid Rachmed get the iouks ready. At 7 a.m., the thermometer is fifteen degrees below zero, which will show how cold the night was. For want of a minimum thermometer, it is impossible to say what the temperature was. So many of our instruments have got broken.

At 8 a.m., it is 9½ degrees below zero in the shade, and only seven above it in the sun.

At 8.25 a.m., it is four degrees below zero in the shade, and only sixteen above it in the sun.

At 9 a.m., it is 9¼ degrees above zero in the shade, and four degrees of frost in the sun; while at 9.40 a.m., just as we start, the cold, for some peculiar reason, increases.

The camels having been heavily loaded, despite the remonstrances of their owners, who assert that their animals are scarcely capable of carrying the iouk of a horse, we make our way towards the eastern extremity of the basin.

We pass over the frozen surface of the lake, the edges of which have a great many cracks, and in some of the hollows there is ice, and in others salt, which might be mistaken for hoar-frost. Then we get into the steppe, and further on the sand begins again; this sand being at the bed of a watercourse which is formed by the melting of the snow.

But our caravan proceeds so slowly that the tardiness must be intentional. From the moment that they saw their beasts of burden being loaded, the Kirghiz had shown manifest signs of ill-humour, and Menas asks me what is to be done; whether he is to let them have the whip. As he is speaking to me, they come to a full stop, and a man, who has ridden up to them on a camel, has an animated conversation with them.

PAMIR HORSE.

This man then comes up to us, and, getting off his camel, kneels down a few paces in front of us and gazes earnestly in our faces.

We ask him what he wants, and he replies—

"I have come to tell you that you cannot go any further until you have received the authorization of the Governor of Kashgar."

"Why?"

"Because I am the chief of the Karauls, and such is the order given me. A few years ago, my predecessor facilitated the journey of some Russians, and he was severely punished, being banished with all his family."

"But we are not Russians."

"What are you, then?"

"We are Feringhis, who are travelling to gain instruction. If we were soldiers, we could understand your opposing our passage, but we are men of peace, and you have no more right to stop us than you have to stop the traders. Moreover, to set you at ease, we may tell you that the *Daotaï* (governor) of Kashgar knows who we are and what we want. The daotaï has not given you any orders about us, so that we are not doing any harm. Moreover, we are not attempting to hide ourselves. We have too much baggage for you to imagine that we are dishonest men. Have we not sent to hire camels? Have we stolen anything? Who complains of us? We do not know anything about you. Where are your papers?"

As he made no reply, we went on to say—

"Accompany us to the end of our stage. You will take some tea with us, and eat sugar. We will show you our papers with Mussulman seals, and if that does not satisfy you, we will await the orders of the daotaï, and you will see that he will send soldiers to cut your head off for having stopped us without a motive."

He still made no answer, and just then our caravan came up, Rachmed abusing the Kirghiz in the strongest language because they will not quicken the pace of their camels, asserting that they will unload them and that they are not fit to travel. Rachmed is eager to know whether he may not beat them, but I urge him to forbear, at all events till this evening. We march along at a desperately slow pace, Sadik being very gloomy, while Satti-Kul still has that jaunty look which has already excited my suspicion, nor has his cousin Djuma-Bi the modest air he had yesterday. After three hours' march, Djuma-Bi wants us to encamp among five or six tents inhabited by the Karauls, upon the ground that there is no grass further on. We refuse his offered hospitality, and select a place on the plain, about a mile off, whence we can see in all directions. Although the road is perfectly clear, the wind having swept away all the snow, the Kirghiz take an hour to do this mile. They take too great an advantage of our good nature, and our men are furious.

The tent has scarcely been put up, and the felt laid down, when the chief of the Karauls arrives in the company of Djuma-Bi and ten hang-dog looking individuals, one of whom is smaller than the rest—doubtless bent by study, for he is presented to us as a mollah—and it is to him that we show our papers. The unloaded animals are at once driven off in the direction of the mountain, and will be found again when they are required.

We offer tea to the principal men, including the malbâti, and the same conversation ensues. Some of them are inclined to be insolent, seeing that we are so very forbearing. They are very anxious to see our papers, so we unfold a passport, and show to the mollah the Persian visa, and then a letter from Muchir-Daoulet (the shah's prime minister), which we found answer its purpose in Khorassan. It is written in Persian, but after conning over it for a long time, he at last came on the word Khorassan, and said—

" This is a Mussulman document."

" Now are you satisfied?" I said to the chief. " You won't stand in the way of our hiring camels now! You must be convinced that we are honourable men."

The Karaul-Begi seems to be convinced, and promises us some camels for to-morrow. We discuss the price with Djuma-

Bi, and come to an understanding, so that everything seems to be going very smoothly. Some friends of Satti-Kul come to see him, and when they leave, they take with them a bundle containing his clothes. This looks a bad sign, and the fellow seems unusually lively. He undertakes to get us some beasts of burden, and we send him to take a turn round by the tents, where some of these animals are lying under cover. He says that he shall be able to get some there, and we send Sadik with him, impressing upon the latter that he must keep his weather-eye open. We then go to bed.

April 2nd.

Early in the morning, we find Djuma-Bi, with the owners of the camels which we used yesterday, the Karaul chief, and his men. Satti-Kul and Sadik come in and tell us that they have only been able to find two camels, which will be brought to us almost immediately.

We remind the Karaul chief of his promise made yesterday, that everything should be ready. He must have told us an untruth therefore. We ask him why the camels have not arrived, and, after a little hesitation, he replies—

"I cannot order the Kirghiz to supply you with camels until I have myself received orders to do so from the Daotai of Kashgar. I can only advise you to wait for a fortnight, when the weather will be better, and all your wishes will be attended to at once."

I then ask the Kirghiz and Djuma-Bi whether they will let us have their camels. They reply—

"We cannot do so without an order of the Karaul chief. Moreover, you ought to pay us. How can you expect us to serve you when you have not paid us the money you owe us since yesterday."

I explain that I had intended to pay the whole at the same time, as I had reckoned upon Djumbi still serving us.

We take the iambas out of the stocking which we use as a purse, and weigh out the silver bars in some scales. The men put this in their belts which they tie in a knot, and then they get up and go off laughing at us. Menas calls them back and invites them to drink a cup of tea, which they do with a grin.

I then address myself to the Karaul chief, and beg of him to procure us the camels he has promised us. He says nothing, and gets up to go away with the rest of his men. Thereupon, I tell

THE PAYMENT.

Menas to seize one of them by the collar and drive him off with the butt-end of his musket towards the mountain, where the camels are, and bring them in at any cost.

I snatch the chief's cudgel out of his hand and belabour him as well as Djuma-Bi with it, while the rest of our men point their revolvers and rifles at them to quell any attempt at resistance. They are told that the first who attempts to fly will have a bullet put into him. Menas goes off, driving one of the men before him, and Sadik follows on horseback, for we must strike while the iron is hot. In the meanwhile, we get the baggage ready, but the tent must not be struck till the last minute, for as long as they see it standing, those who are watching us from a distance will think that we are not starting, and that nothing abnormal is going on.

Half an hour later, Menas and Sadik come in with some camels.

I need hardly say that our would-be captors, finding that the tables have been turned on them, look very foolish. They do not even think of finishing their tea. We shall not soon forget the faces of the two who got the worst beating, with their heads

ORNAMENTS AND ARKAR HORNS.

hung down, making small sand-heaps, like children playing by the sea-shore.

Once the camels have come in, we load them as quickly as possible, and when the baggage has got on some way ahead, we wish them good-bye, and trot off after our caravan as quickly as possible.

Satti-Kul has gone off with a very long face, and when we overtake him, he tells us that he has sent a man to Tashkurgan— the traces of this man's camel are still visible in the snow—and that an attempt will be made to stop us in the valley of Ak-Su. We shall see.

On looking back, we see some men going to talk with the

chief of the Karauls. We then ascend the valley of the Kara-Su, following a southerly course, passing several *barkhanes* (sand hills), which are driven before the wind from place to place. At five o'clock, we encamp at Chatiput, in a well-sheltered hollow, at a point where several valleys meet. Before reaching the end of this stage, I have to abandon my horse.

CHATTPUT.

CHAPTER XIII.

THE PAMIR (*continued*).

Hostility of the natives—A friend of Sadik—Upon the banks of the Ak-Su, or the Oxus—News from Kunjut—The Kirghiz make off—A funereal monument—An apparition—A derelict—The debts of Satti-Kul, our guide—His flight—Refusal to assist us or sell us any provisions—Our "brother" Abdullah-Khan—The white slave—An excess of obedience—Abandoned tents—A friend—Enemies—Requisitions—The further end of the Ak-Su valley.

I WILL now hurry my narrative to a more rapid conclusion, abridging the account of days which did not bring any novel feature with them, and putting a curb upon my recollections which might risk being prolix.

April 3rd.

Last evening, our camp-fire attracted a dozen or so of Kirghiz, whose tents are raised behind some sheltering hills. They had shown great affability, and several of them had recognized the ill-favoured Satti-Kul. We had offered them some tea, and they had told us that the Kunjut had for some little time been Feringhi, that is to say, English. We hope that such may prove to be the case. Moreover, the bi (chief) promised us some camels for to-morrow, without fail.

Upon waking, I find that not only have these camels not come, but those of the day before have also disappeared, and all of the Kirghiz with them.

During the night they have made a clean sweep of it, and the bi, who has promised so much, has gone too. I then send Menas in search of Satti-Kul, who had asked permission to go and see some of his relatives, from whom he would be able to get all the beasts of burden we require. He has now been gone two hours, and when he went he was riding one of our horses, while a friend was on the back of another. Perhaps we shall see nothing more of one or the other.

Menas returns with a yak, which he says that he found grazing, and adds that Satti-Kul is following with a fresh horse. I then take a turn with Menas to the adjoining tents, all the occupants of which say, in reply to our inquiries about the bi, that they do not know where he is, and that, moreover, they do not belong to the district. We find a camel, and a brother of the camel-drivers we had yesterday brings us two yaks. The owners of the camel and the yak which we had taken possession of come to claim their animals, whereupon we insist upon their loading them and driving them for us, giving them the choice between a ball from a revolver or a beating, and money in return for their services. We shall henceforth be obliged to requisition all we want, as the natives will neither sell nor hire us anything. These people first try to get all they can out of us and then refuse to render us the slightest service.

Satti-Kul, who is unquestionably very sulky and ill-disposed, arrives after keeping us waiting three hours. Rachmed and his

THE START FROM CHAITPUT.

three companions are anxious to give him a beating, but I prevent this, as he is the only one who knows the road, and until we reach the valley of the Oxus, we must humour him. It is evident that he is watching for an opportunity of making off, so we must keep a sharp look-out on him.

We start at once, crossing the creek to the west of which we have bivouacked, and make south by the valley of Chattput, which is about one thousand yards wide and very sandy, the tips of mica-schiste rock protruding just above the sand. From the outset, we come upon barkhanes of sand moving north, though the varying of the wind prevents them travelling very fast.

After three hours' march, we descend into an amphitheatre by way of some sandhills buried beneath the snow, and we shape our course to the south-west.

This valley is also sandy, of about the same width as the previous one, with very little snow. We follow it for three hours, as far as the point at which it narrows and takes the name of Koch-Aguil. The westerly wind interferes with our progress not a little. In the valley there is a great accumulation of sand, especially to the left, that is to the west, and one might imagine that it was about to scale the mountain slopes, whereas in reality it is tumbling down from them.

Before sunset, Rachmed comes up with us, grumbling about the yaks, which he says are all hair and no legs. They move very slowly.

I tell him that we ought to be satisfied, as we have got safely down.

He answers, "Yes, about two feet," and points out the place where we had better bivouac. Shaking his fist at the wind and cursing it fearfully, he says, " I have still got my stomach full of it, and if I had not kept my teeth closed, the soul would have been blown out of my body. What a sweet spot! No grass! No water! Sand, and plenty of snow. What a fine laïlag!" Being thirsty, he puts some snow into his mouth, and adds, "And to think that at Beï-Kongur" (the residence of his tribe), "there is now abundance of everything—grass for the stock, plenty of water, and on the mountain enough garlic to keep a man for six weeks without eating anything else. That is the country to live in."

Sadik feels himself at home; he has come here once before from the Ak-Su, and he has a friend in the neighbourhood who has rendered him a great service, and who knows how to make gun barrels. Upon the Pamir every Kirghiz has his matchlock.

"What service did he do you, Sadik?"

"One day, when I had gone to the neighbourhood of the Kara-Kul with the intention of making a baranta, I came upon some sheep belonging to men of his tribe, and, to tell you the truth, I seized some of them. I was returning, driving about twenty of these sheep before me, when I was caught by the men to whom they belonged. They seized me and took me back to their aoul, meaning to despatch me, when the Teït who is near here—there are none but Teïts in this country—recognized me. We had made barantas together in the direction of the Wakhan, at the time that I had gone off with the brother of Batir-Beg, and we had preserved pleasant recollections of each other. He accordingly intervened in my favour and had me released. I am going to pay him a visit, and when I tell him that you will pay him well, he will come. I shall sleep at his place, and I warrant you that I shall return to-morrow with the yaks we require."

We give Sadik a few pinches of tea for his friend, and two or three lumps of sugar, and I call out to him, as he starts, not to come back without the yaks, and that if he fails, after all his fine promises, he had better not come back at all.

When it is quite dark, at nine o'clock, the wind drops and the thermometer marks only sixteen degrees of frost, so we think the temperature is delightful and stand at the entrance to our tent to enjoy the cool evening air. At the bivouac this morning (8 a.m.) we had twenty-five degrees of frost. Summer is evidently coming.

April 4th.

Sadik arrives about 7.30 a.m. with two camels, a yak, and two Kirghiz, father and son. These two friends of his are little men, with very hooked noses protruding from a regular Mongol face. We load the beasts and pack off the camel-drivers of the day before, whom we had taken care to keep for fear Sadik should not succeed.

We travel in a southerly direction, following the small stream which passes to the west of this valley, suddenly becoming very narrow. In an hour and a half, having climbed a stony hill, we descend into the snow-covered valley of the Ak-Su, reaching a plain about six miles in diameter, shut in by a belt of snow-capped mountains. The horizon is rather broader. We make our way through the snow, still travelling south. Approaching the river, the snow almost disappears, and we descend a very stony piece of ground to the edge of the frozen river, which we cross over, and encamp at the further end of one of the bends which it makes on its course through the plain. The Ak-Su, when frozen, is from thirty to sixty feet broad, while its bed, distinctly marked by the lofty banks, is from three hundred and fifty to seven hundred feet wide. Satti-Kul says, that when the river is swollen by the rains, the whole of this bed is filled.

Upon the other side of the river we see two shepherds, armed with muskets, keeping watch over some sheep. We are always glad to catch sight of anything which will make mutton, and we send Satti-Kul to speak to them.

We inform Menas and Rachmed that this river is the Amu-Darya, which they have already seen at Chardjui, Chur-Tepe, and Khiva, and this piece of news delights them, and they salute the Ak-Su. Rachmed is anxious to break the ice where it is thinnest, and to throw into the water two branches of trees, a coin, two dried apricots, etc., and to pronounce a few words by way of a charm.

We, too, are glad to be upon the banks of the Ak-Su, or the

ENCAMPMENT UPON THE OXUS.

Oxus. For the first time we feel as if we were on a main-road. We are isolated, it is true, but we could, if necessary, descend into Bokhara. At the Kara-Kul and Rang-Kul we were in the plain, too, but one had the feeling of being shut in and of having fallen into some profound abyss.

So, without losing a minute, we sent to draw some water at the watering-place which has been cut out near the bank for the sheep, and we drink it with relish.

To the south-east, we saw the defile of Ak-Tach, and that is whence the wind comes of a night. Opposite the entrance to our tent, to the north-west, is the pass of Ak-Djilgua, whence starts the summer road to the Rang-Kul. Around us is plenty of grass—last year's grass—for our horses, and roots of one kind and another. We give our horses very little barley, and at the ordinary feeding time, one of them comes up to the camp-fire and neighs very plaintively, as much as to say, "Are you going to deprive us of our nosebag while you yourselves are enjoying the delicious water of the Ak-Su." The truth is, that we must husband the excellent Ferghana barley until we have to load our horses heavily. So we drive the poor brute off.

April 5th.

To the north-east I can see the back of the Tagharma, I say the back, because from this date we shall be turning our backs on him, and very glad we are that it is so. We are gradually making our way to warmer countries; yesterday, at eight o'clock, there were twenty-five degrees of frost; to-day, at the same hour there are only twelve.

At ten o'clock, we start, with snow nearly two feet deep, and we encamp at Ustik-Dalasu, a place which has been visited by some English, as we are told by an old man with a hooked nose, who gives himself out as the bi of the district. This chief comes to pay us a visit with a bag full of plants and roots on his back, and he makes a seat of it while he is talking to us. He at once recognizes Satti-Kul, and this puts him at his ease with us. He tells us that a little further on the road is a bad one, that all the stock has died this season, and that they have not a camel or a yak capable of going fifty yards.

He adds that the Kunjut is independent, and gives us the following account of what has occurred in that region. The young khan, having killed his father, sent ambassadors to the

Daotaï of Kashgar to say, "If I have killed my father, it is because he wanted to hand over our country to the Inglis (English), and because I wish to be friends with the Emperor of Tsin (China)." The envoys then asked the Daotaï whether their master had done right, and he replied, of course, in the affirmative. Thereupon, he gave orders that the men from the Kunjut should be received with great hospitality, and sent them home with many bars of silver and valuable stuffs as presents. Thus the Kunjut

AK-TACH (WHITE STONE).

is still independent. Last year, the English passed by way of Basaï-Gumbaz with Indian soldiers and men from the Kunjut.

At the present moment there are some Afghans at Ak-Tach. They have come from Kashgar, and have lost about forty horses on their way by Nisa-Tach. They are waiting for fine weather before continuing their journey to Badakshan. This is a significant piece of news for us.

The bi winds up his gossip by telling us that the Teït are very badly off this year, that they have lost nearly all their stock, and that the situation of their tents is so bad that they will have to shift. They have accordingly sent one of their number to Tashkurgan to complain to the beg of their distress. The beg has taken their prayer into favourable consideration, and he is expected to-morrow, or the day after, with an escort of sixty or eighty men, to examine into the justice of their demands. This is said with a view to intimidating us.

Thereupon the bi whispers for a little to his cousin, Satti-Kul, and then makes off. We do not see a single camel anywhere near, and the two or three yaks which are roaming about near

THE TAGHARMA, SEEN FROM THE OXUS.

the bi's tent seem to be devoid of all strength. Probably the animals which are in good condition have been hidden away somewhere. Two of the bi's children come to see us, a boy and a girl, and the latter, whose brother follows her with manifest hesitation, says that she saw the canvas of our tent, which was so different from that of her father's, that she had come to see what it could be.

Menas is busy breaking sugar, and our little visitors watch him with great interest, and after they have tasted a few grains and made sure that it is not white stone, they ask for a lump. Menas pretends not to hear, and asks the girl if there are any camels about. She seems very wide-awake, and makes an evasive answer, saying she does not know. Then, having got tired of watching Menas breaking the sugar, she makes a sign to her brother, who is not nearly so bold as she is, but quite as dirty, and off they go. These children are washed the day of their birth, but not afterwards. They were as much interested in the sugar as any European child would be in seeing an Esquimaux eating whale, or an African swallowing grasshoppers.

Upon the 6th of April, we leave Ustik without any assistance,

MENAS AND THE KIRGHIZ CHILDREN.

and we have discharged Sadik's friend. All the Kirghiz are in hiding, and their animals have disappeared, with the exception of two or three female yaks big with young. We encounter a great deal of snow and a lot of arkars, all out of range; but upon the ice of the Ak-Su we see the traces of a recent tragedy, a good deal of blood and remnants of skin, where some wolves had devoured an arkar.

We encamp at a place where there is no snow, a pasturage which Satti-Kul calls Dja, and we spend the next day (the 7th) there to rest the horses.

April 8th.

We start for Ak-Tach, winding about in the deep snow along the high banks of the Ak-Su, keeping as near as possible to the mountain spurs on the right bank, our guiding-star being the rock of Ak-Tach, which keeps appearing and disappearing, gradually growing in size each time we see it. Suddenly, in a corner of the valley, in the direction which we are following, an extraordinary sight greets our eyes, viz. a number of walls and cupolas in course of construction. We ask Satti-Kul what they are, and he replies, not without a certain amount of pride, that they are monuments erected in the grand cemetery of the Teïts, to the memory of members belonging to illustrious and powerful families. They are meghuils in the Kirghiz style, cones erected upon four walls.

The only building which man has had the energy to construct here is one to commemorate death, and this, as it should be, in a country where life is a strange and almost inexplicable exception, where man only manages to vegetate because he is an animal strenuously resolved to live. Or perhaps the inhabitants of the Pamir, crushed by the forces of nature, understand better than any one else that he is condemned to die, and says to himself, "Why should I take the trouble of going to die elsewhere?"

The tumuli are built south-west to north-east, so that the dead may have their faces turned towards the holy city. They extend around four mausoleums made of earth, about double the height of an *ouï* (felt tent), and with a frontage of about thirty feet. The cupolas are pointed, and the architecture very simple, as there are no materials handy to attempt anything ambitious. Moreover, if a higher building had been erected, the wind, which is the terror of the Pamir, would soon have brought it to the ground.

At the four corners of the largest of the mausoleums, a rude attempt has been made to carve pigeons; but still one can see that they are meant for pigeons. The snow, driving in through the door, has covered the tomb upon which the horns of arkars have been placed, these being the only "flowers" which can be had for weaving into wreaths.

Two tugs are swinging to and fro like the wooden carvings meant to represent grapes which one sees hanging over the doorway of inns. These tugs, made out of the tails of yaks and rags, are encrusted in snow, which has melted and frozen again, and they look as if they had been carved out of marble.

CEMETERY OF KARA-KIRGHIZ.

At the end of the humbler tombs are some stones sunk into the earth. Some of them have a sort of railing round them, formed of stakes bound together by woollen cords.

As the snow is deep and it is difficult to advance, we make for the Ak-Su, which is close by, and continue our journey over the ice. To our right, the sides of the steep banks are almost clear of snow, and thin streams of water, trickling from the crevices, find their way on to the surface, and get frozen as soon as the sun has gone down. Passing over this ice of recent formation, it cracked beneath our feet, for there were only thin layers of it, but there was no risk of getting a cold bath, for the stratum beneath was thick enough to bear almost any weight. As the river bends about a good deal, we again climb the bank to our right, and then we find ourselves amid the rocks which are scattered along the stone wall known as the Ak-Tach (White Stone).

Just as my horse is picking his way over the rough ground, with a bitterly cold wind blowing, I see a woman, like an old witch, roaming about among the large stones. She stops short and looks stolidly at me. She must be the sorceress of the Pamir. My sight is very weak, and I cannot at first make out her features, with or without my spectacles. She is very upright, though of short stature, and she wears, with her sheepskins, a white head-dress to distinguish her sex. There are two holes where her eyes should be, and her nose is not visible. Around her lie the carcases of horses, the gaping skeletons of camels, and heads of sheep, with the teeth set and grinning. She looks like some mummified minister of death, but for all that she is a living old woman of the Kirghiz tribe.

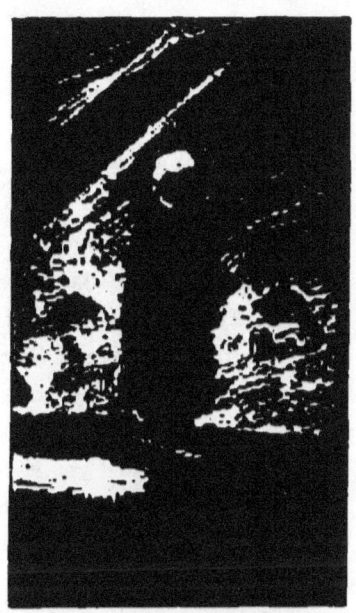

KIRGHIZ WOMAN OF THE PAMIR.

We come to a number of tents erected on the sheltered ground, with men, women, children, dogs and horses, perhaps about thirty in all. Satti-Kul wants us to encamp among the charnel-houses which form the gardens to these tents. But I propose that we should go further along the valley, to the bottom of the Ak-Tach, to some peat bogs, where there is not so much snow. I had scarcely told Satti-Kul to proceed and not get into conversation with the inquisitive people, who had come trooping round us, when I heard some one calling to me "Bradar!" ("Brother!") in Persian.

Looking round, I see a man wearing, like us, the *malakai* (sheepskin headdress), but with a handsome Afghan face and regular features. After an exchange of salutations, he says—

"Where are you going?"

"To Hindostan; and where do you come from?"

"From Kashgar, by Tagharma, where I lost all my horses in the snow, with the exception of the six you see, and they are not fit for anything."

"Where are you going?"

"To Cabul, by the Badakshan. I am taking *khame* (a rough cotton stuff) from Kashgar, and *bang* (hachisch). I have twenty iouks of cotton and five of haschisch left. I have a companion who is conveying Thibet goats' wool for the making of costly shawls."

"How comes it that you have taken this road?"

"It is the first time we have passed this way in winter. When we left Kashgar, we did not know that the route was such a difficult one, but as soon as we had got into the mountain the snow got deeper and deeper, and when we reached Ak-Tach, we had six horses left and all our merchandise was littered along the route. We asked the Kirghiz of Ak-Tach to go and fetch them. They refused at first, and then we bargained with them for three days, when——"

But the place is not a suitable one for conversation, as the wind is bitterly cold, and then I don't know who this man may be. He comes running after us and asks if we have any tea, to which Rachmed of course replies in the negative.

We pitch our tent far enough from the "White Stone" not to be crushed by any fragments which may fall from it.

The inhabitants of Ak-Tach come and examine us in turns, and many of them recognize Satti-Kul, who does not seem particularly overjoyed at seeing them again, as several are his creditors or his enemies. An old man from the neighbourhood of Andamane, who appears at the head of five or six men of his tribe and acts as their spokesman, reminds Satti-Kul of several disagreeable matters, and the latter appears to have dropped into a regular wasps' nest.

"Did you not formerly steal two camels from so and so. You never paid for the mares you bought of the other. You went off with a third's stallion and sold him at Rang-Kul. You are credited with having made off with the daughter of the man at Basai-Gumbaz, and so on."

Satti-Kul listened to the enumeration of his misdeeds with the impassibility of the most hardened offender, and sipped quietly his cup of tea while his judicial antecedents were being set before him. He hardly deigned to make a reply, and only gave an underhand look now and again.

Then the old man pointed to one of his companions and said—

"Can you deny that you owe this man an iamba?"

Satti-Kul at length opened his mouth and replied—

"I don't deny that I have an account to settle. But the question is which of us is indebted to the other. To-day, I am very busy, but if you will come to-morrow, we will take some stones to count. We shall see which of us has some stones left."

I ought to have explained how these savages count, and you will see that in the west of Europe we started from the same principle, and that the calculating tables recently employed in France are not dissimilar as to method. Calculation is derived from calculus (small stone), and it was with stones that sums in addition and subtraction were made before the use of figures.

Thus, when two Kirghiz have an account to settle, they meet in the presence of witnesses, and according as one of them acknowledges his indebtedness, he places before his creditor a stone representing a fixed sum, or rather quantity—a sheep or a camel, for instance. Then the same individual removes alternately a stone from each heap, and the one who has any stones left before him, is the one to whom a balance is owing. Sometimes the stones are set out in rows, instead of in heaps, and it can be seen at a glance that the one with the longest row is the one who has a balance in his favour. This is what Satti-Kul proposes to do with his creditors.

Just then, a flock of sheep passes close to our encampment, and Satti-Kul is told to bargain with the owner, but, after a lengthy argument, it turns out that he has got hold of the wrong man, and when the real owner comes up, he declines to sell. But in the meanwhile, Rachmed has killed one of the sheep, much to his disgust, for he declines to receive any money for it. But Rachmed says that he is safe to come and fetch it to-morrow morning.

We have a long talk with Abdullah-Khan, the merchant whom we had met just before, and he completes his story of how the Kirghiz, after refusing to go and fetch his goods, had only consented to do so upon payment of a most exorbitant sum. Having made a reconnaissance for himself, and seen that the valley was buried beneath the snow, he had determined to await finer weather before continuing his journey into the Wakhan, which is in the power of the Afghans, and where he is sure of finding beasts of burden. " Though the men of this land," he adds, "are not very pleasant to deal with."

We give him a little tea, as he has been out of it for a week, and we question him as to the Kunjut route, but he does not know much about it, except that a pass near Basaï-Gumbaz leads to it, and that there is another road further on.

For the matter of that, there is no lack of passes, but they are closed. Not far from where we are, is that of Bik-Bel, but we should require good animals and good guides to recommence the struggles of the Alaï and the Kizil-Art, and these we have not got. The bis of Ak-Tach have already forbidden the natives to supply us with anything, and there is no faith to be placed upon their promises to supply us with the barley and flour we are quite prepared to pay for.

If the people of Ak-Tach were at all reasonable, it would not be by any means a bad place to stay at, for there is water to be had in the peat bogs, and if the grass is not very good, there is plenty of it. Moreover, the cold has suddenly become much less intense, and at 7.25 p.m. there are only two or three degrees of frost.

April 9th.

In spite of, or rather because of, the promises made the day before, we see no sign of any camel or yak. Satti-Kul started off last evening upon the pretext that he was going to pass the night at an aoul where he had been promised two camels, and it so happened that he was riding our best horse. There is no sign of him or the horse the next morning, when the weather is fine but much colder (fourteen degrees of frost at 8 a.m.), with a south-east wind which blows down from the sources of the Oxus.

We send Sadik to the bis, more as a matter of form than anything else, to ask what they have decided to do, and to request them to pay us a visit. They do not come themselves, merely telling Sadik that they are about to send out some horsemen to ascertain the depth of the snow. We had better wait, they say, till these men come back, and when we know what the route is like, they will provide us with camels, horses, provisions, etc. They add that it will be a great pity if our lordships do not wait at Ak-Tach for fine weather, instead of risking the loss of our horses.

Abdu-Rasoul comes into the camp at about the same time, and says that he can glean no tidings of Satti-Kul. Menas and Sadik then mount their horses and go off in quest of him, but they return about noon, saying that they have discovered the tracks of his horse near the Ak-Su. These tracks, however, were made yesterday, and they conclude that he has taken to flight from his creditors.

We now remain only seven. The route is an easy one to follow up to the Wakhan frontier, where we shall be able to get a

THE HANGING WALL AT AK-TACH.

guide if necessary, so the loss would not be a very great one if he had not taken the best of our horses.

The Afghan trader comes to see us, accompanied by two of his muleteers, who are Andidjanis, as the people of the Ferghana are styled in Kashgar. They are natives of Osch, and we have a talk to them about their native place. If the horses they have left were in better condition, they would accompany us as far as the Wakhan. These men advise us to make for Andaman, which is the name given to the region where the Oxus takes its source, and where the Kirghiz have a winter encampment. There we shall be better able to get means of transport. They also advise us to be on our guard against the people of the Pamir, who are the biggest thieves they ever met.

Abdullah-Khan quite coincides in their views, and he believes that we shall get barley at Andaman; at all events, we are sure to do so in Wakhan. We speak to him about the khan of the Kunjut, whom he describes as a beggar and a brigand, who robs and

TYPES OF KIRGHIZ KHANS.

murders the weak, and goes whining for alms to the powerful. To the Afghans, he says, " I am Afghan, make me a present," and the same to the Chinese, the English, or the men of Kashmir, as the case may be.

We purchase from Abdullah-Khan some cotton stuffs which will be useful to us on the road, and we pay him in imperial polls, for he is familiar with Russian gold. He gets us a man who is going to Andaman to see a sick relative, and he will show us the way. Abdullah-Khan, after wishing us good-bye, spends part of the night beside the camp-fire, talking with Menas about Afghanistan, Hindostan, the Caucasus, Persia and Stamboul. While they are talking, the other men come in, and say that they have passed a charming evening in ladies' society and eaten a lot of wild goats' flesh, which was excellent.

April 10th.

At 8 a.m., there are fourteen degrees of frost, with a southeast wind. One of the bis has come to see us, being attracted by the loading of the horses. He is a former Karaul chief at Ak-Tach, and he says that if he had his way, he would let us have what we require, but that he is not master. But, polite as he is, we request him to begone. We would have taken what we wanted by force, were we not afraid that Sadik and Abdu-Rasoul, whom we shall be sending back when we reach the Kunjut frontier, would be made to suffer for it. When we have got further on, we shall not stand on any ceremony.

We start at ten o'clock, following the left bank of the Ak-Su. The snow is very deep, quite filling the bed of the river. In places, there is a stream of water from the glaciers, where the current is very deep, and as there is of course no snow here, we can measure its depth in other places, there being at least eighteen feet. These pools of water are haunted by water-fowl named dournas, a sort of cross between the duck and the cormorant, which we found very palatable.

We do a good part of the journey on foot, and unload the horses, so as to rest them. Our guide can hardly drag himself along, and, after stopping several times, takes off his belt and pushes it down his throat to make himself sick. This appears to relieve him, though he is still as pale as death. Menas gets him to tell his story, which is a very simple one.

"Before starting this morning, a good deal of millet porridge remained in the pot, and Sadik told me that I had better finish it. I had too much, and that made me ill. Now I am better."

We laugh to death at this; but the guide, who cannot understand why we laugh, says, "But as Sadik," (the father, as he calls him), "told me to eat it, what was I to do?"

Soon after this, some arkars appeared on the hills, about two hundred and fifty yards away. We wounded two, and thanks to our dogs, we got one of them. I had to run about three hundred yards to try and prevent the dogs from tearing its skin, when I

YOUNG ARKAR KILLED NEAR AK-TACH.

suddenly felt a sharp pain in the chest. I have always been very strong there, so I hope that this is nothing.

After crossing the Ak-Su, which is visible in places, but in others is hidden by the snow, we halt on the banks of the river, at Kizil-Rabat. It is just three o'clock, and we are prostrated by the torrid and blinding heat. At 3.30 p.m., the thermometer marks ninety-nine degrees in the sun, and forty-one degrees in the shade, so that there would soon be a thaw if this weather lasted. But at seven o'clock, there are five and a half degrees of frost, and at ten o'clock, nine degrees, with a clear sky and no wind.

April 11th.

At 7.35 a.m., there are twenty-two degrees of frost; at 8 a.m., thirteen degrees; and at 10.15 a.m., fourteen degrees, with a northeast breeze. The night has been very cold, and we all complain of having slept very badly and of violent headaches.

We start at 10.15 a.m., the snow being very deep, and the horses slipping up at every turn. We see no sign of any inhabitants, and have to come down from the heights into the valley, because the snow is so deep. Our guide endeavours to make off, but when I bring my rifle to bear on him, he comes back fast enough.

At the foot of the hills, we come upon several abandoned tents with a number of dead animals all around them. Riding up to one of these tents, my horse starts back in terror, and I cannot get him to advance again. So handing him to Pepin, who has just been making a sketch, I go up to the tents, and find that their owners, before going off, have tied up to the pegs a number of dead goats, which have been reduced to mummies by the frost, and grin in a most diabolical manner. They appear to have been hideous enough to frighten the very birds of prey, which have not attempted to touch them.

Raising a flap of the tent, which is white with the droppings of the birds of prey, a couple of flies come out with a buzz, and these are the first insects we have seen for a long time. Inside the tent are saddles, rolls of felt, skins, and all the utensils of a nomad. The only trace on the ground is that of wolves, but there are a few stones which have evidently been used for domestic purposes, for crushing bones, corn, etc.

Some of the dead animals have evidently been killed by the hand of man, for they have been skinned and their heads cut off. But others have died of cold and hunger, and those which have died of congestion have their stomachs full, while the remainder

COMING UPON AN ABANDONED GUN.

look quite pinched and starved. A crow comes and perches upon the rock above, ready for his meal, and the sun shines over this lugubrious scene as over all else.

We continue our course westward, following the Ak-Su, which enters by a narrow channel into a gradually broadening valley where there is a lake more than half a mile wide. We cross it upon the ice, and as we are doing so, one of our horses drops, never to rise again. Capus also has to leave his behind. We encamp at the extremity of the lake, upon the summit of some stony ridges, which we only reach after great difficulty, owing to the accumulation of snow. We have been six hours on the march.

We are upon the edge of one of the great reservoirs of the Ak-Su, and have ascended nearly seven hundred feet since our last bivouac. This evening we feel shut in, as it were, for the mountains close the horizon, though here and there are gaps through which the stars can be seen like fires lighted on the mountain sides in Switzerland the evening before a festival. The scenery is less polar than what we have been accustomed to.

April 12th.

We left Irmenatag at eleven, amid sleet and snow, and we separate from one another after having crossed the Ak-Su and climbed some hills. The snow is still coming down so thick that we cannot see the road, and I follow Menas and the guide. The road is so bad, and the snowstorm so blinding, that the horses cannot keep their legs, and we have to halt and unload them. Menas is furious because he cannot keep his legs and stumbles about, but at last we get down again on to the frozen Ak-Su, where there is less snow, and eventually reach Ghuzalane and encamp upon an elevated piece of ground.

We are all in a sad plight, with noses bleeding, heads aching, and ears singing. I hear the cry of some suksurs overhead, and shoot at them, but they are out of range. Nothing could be grander, however, than the sunset, after this sunless day, and there is a gleam of gold over the mountain tops as night sets in.

The early part of the night is cloudy, but about eleven the sky clears. We sleep badly, feeling half suffocated.

April 13th.

The snow, which had melted on the surface yesterday, has frozen again, and it shines like a looking-glass.

CAMP OF KIZIL-KORUM.

With a south-west breeze, there are sixty-seven degrees at 9.30 a.m. in the sun, and seven degrees of frost in the shade; while at eleven, there are seventy-seven degrees in the sun, and about thirty-five in the shade.

All the men complain of having been so cold during the night, and this is because the droppings and roots which we have to burn are damp from the half thaw of the day before.

We march for about five and a half hours, and encamp at Kizil-Korum, where we meet with some yourtes. A man named

Sarik-Makmed sells us a sheep. He formerly inhabited the Alaï, and we have no difficulty in getting provisions through him. He promises also to let us have two camels and a horse, which are all that the winter has left him with. He declares that he will never pass another winter here, and he invites our men to sup with him. He is living on the left bank of the Ak-Su, with four or five men of his tribe, and is at daggers drawn with some men on the right bank. We give a little present to his son, to whom he seems to be much attached, for he kisses him as he fastens his pelisse and says—

"You see, it is my youngest. Return to your tent, my dear child. The sun is setting, and you will be cold."

April 14th.

A day of rest and high feeding. Abdur-Rasul makes a sausage, and he is quite an artist.

To-morrow, we shall make a start with Sarik-Mahmed's camels. He says—

"I am not afraid of the Chinese. If I had any barley, I would let you have some. My brother will show you the way. When the Chinese come, I shall be off. I have a friend at Ak-Tach who will let me know in time."

We send back Mirza-Beï, our guide, giving him several pieces of cloth and a little sugar. He is quite happy; and when we remind him of his attack of indigestion, he smiles, and again says—

"How could it be helped? The father (Sadik) told me to eat it all."

April 15th.

Thanks to Sarik-Mahmed, five yaks and a camel are placed at our disposal, and we proceed, amid another fall of snow, to Mus-Kalé, about two hours from here. There is a Kirghiz aoul at this place, and the men assemble and take counsel of their chief, an aged man, who will not interfere, and retires to his tent upon the right bank of the Ak-Su.

I make several proposals to the assembled Kirghiz, but we cannot come to any agreement. We ask for information about the Kunjut route, and a woman, who has been five years a slave in that country, advises us to go by way of Tach-Kupruk.

We have only been able to procure a guide and two camels by threatening to use our rifles and revolvers.

April 16th.

We start at 11.30 a.m. in the snow, and with more falling. Descending into the plain, I follow our old guide, who says that he will take me to a tent where we shall find men and yaks. After two hours' march, he wants us to halt at this tent, which is in a marsh; but we have paid for the stage in advance, and by dint of threats I make him go on. My horse being very tired, I compel him to mount it, and I take his, which is fresher; so he cannot ride off. Then I belabour him with my whip, and regularly drive him up to rejoin the caravan, which has remained on the hillside, where the road is better. Menas, who is with me, seizes two strong-looking yaks, whose owners come running after them. But the latter will have to follow us to our encampment, and then we can arrange with them.

The old guide is very alarmed, and speaks in a whining tone to Sadik, who looks at me and winks, while Abdur-Rasul banters him, and calls him "your lordship," because he is riding my horse.

We bivouac upon the side of the hill, at Tchitab, near the first source of the Oxus, and the owner of one of the yaks soon overtakes us. We ask him to provide us with three yaks and two sheep, and show us the way to the Kunjut. He is quite willing to supply the animals, but as to the Kunjut, he says, "The men of the Kunjut are brigands and thieves. You may as well cut my head off at once. I will go as far as Langar, if you like, and there we shall encounter some Wakhi looking after their flocks."

We agree to this, and pay him in advance for the sheep and for half the hire of the yaks, warning him that if he does not keep

AT THE SOURCES OF THE OXUS.

his word, he had better make off with his tents and flocks, unless he wishes to have a bullet put into him.

Moreover, we put clogs on the legs of the animals we have hired, and we intend to take good care not to let our men get away till we have others in their place, though we treat them as liberally as possible while with us.

The baba receives a nice present; and, after we have given him a good dinner, he feels more at home; a subsequent gift of sugar making him feel so happy, that he promises us a guide—a "divana"—as dervishes are called. Before going home to bed, he salutes us with an "Allah akbar!" of relief, as if not sorry to be off; and with him go the vendor of the sheep and Menas, who, astride a yak, and with his pelisse and Turkoman bonnet, hardly distinguishable from his mount, looks like a centaur.

Menas takes with him a cup to drink the milk which has been promised him, and which he is longing to get, for his stomach is much out of order, and he has a nausea of rice, millet, and even of meat, which, as a rule, he likes so much.

From our tent, pitched at an altitude of thirteen thousand feet, we can see below us the extremity of the frozen lake Tchakmatin-Kul, and beyond the glaciers overhanging it. We are at the extreme west of the Little Pamir, and at the end of the valley where the Ak-Su is fed by an immense reservoir of ice, as it will be later by the snow which is accumulated upon "the roof of the world."

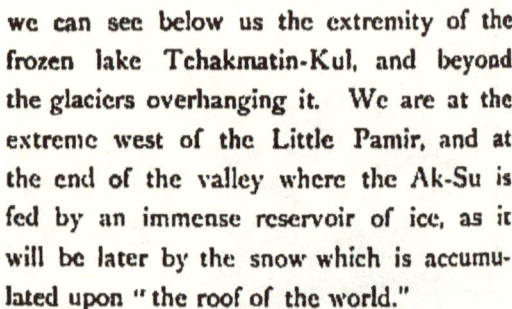

MENAS ON THE YAK.

Part of our task is done. The snow seems less dense westward, and we encamp upon a ledge of rock where there is none. We sniff the odour of the artemisia, that true plant of the steppe, which our horses feed upon greedily, and which reminds us of many another bivouac. In the steppe, we thought they "smelt horrid," but now we think that there is a perfume about them, because they bring us nearer to the goal.

Rachmed, whom that odour has put in a good humour, observes that "it is now six weeks since we left Osch." He feels that it is "the beginning of the end." Let us hope so. In any event, it is the end of the valley of the Ak-Su, with its depressing monotony, of which we have all had enough.

THE GLACIER OF TCHILAR.

CHAPTER XIV.

TOWARDS THE KUNJUT.

The outlaws—An exile—Wakhan-Darya—Langar—Wakhan types—The Kirghiz want to leave us—Diplomacy—We start for the Kunjut with Wakhis—Difficulties; provisions run short; the Wakhis make off—An unsuccessful reconnaissance—We have to return to Langar—Abdullah-Khan turns up again—We send to fetch the abandoned baggage and Menas, who was looking after them—Exacting attitude of the Kirghiz—The Chinese at our heels, but they are too late—A saint.

April 17th.

SNOW is falling at nine o'clock, when there are about two degrees of frost. At ten o'clock, Menas arrives, driving a yak before him, and behind him follow several Kirghiz, with sheep and some more yaks.

The Kirghiz have kept their word, but "not without difficulty," as Menas puts it, for the one whom we had treated with yesterday wanted to give back the money he had received, and not sell or let us anything. We had to resort to promises and threats, undertaking to give him two khames extra to overcome his obstinacy. It appeared afterwards that his wife served our cause, as she was very anxious to have some cloth, and abused her husband in unmeasured terms for letting slip such a good opportunity.

"Was she good-looking, Menas?"

"Good-looking? Ugly as the very devil. No teeth, no hair, wrinkled, dirty, and a scold."

"She received you well, I suppose?"

"She gave me two arkar skins to sleep upon."

"And how about dinner?"

"That was a very simple matter. She kneaded some flour and made it into balls, and then she plunged them into a cauldron of hot water. The water boiled, and then she took out the balls, which we ate with a little salt. This morning she emptied some flour into the same cauldron, added some water, and took a stick to mix it up with. That was all, but fortunately I had already had some curded milk."

"Do you know where this flour comes from?"

"From the Wakhan, where they send to fetch it. I heard them say that their stock was exhausted. They pretended to be very reluctant to carry our baggage, but this was to get us to pay them more, as they are obliged to follow the same road as far as Langar."

"And how about the guide?"

"He is coming on horseback. He will be here directly."

The sheep come in, and they are at once cut up by the vendor himself, who uses the knife with extraordinary skill. He is a small beardless man, with hardly a sound tooth in his head, and a snub nose. One of his assistants is tall and fair, with a rather large eye. A third, although dressed in

Kirghiz fashion, has not at all the Kirghiz type. He speaks to me in Persian, and I look very closely at him, though there is nothing extraordinary in the inhabitants of this corner of the Pamir speaking that language. Many of them even understand the Wakhi dialect. That is easy of explanation, as they are in communication with the caravan men who go in summer from the Kashgar to the Badakshan, most of them being Afghans who can speak Persian. Upon the other hand, they are completely dependent upon the Wakhan, which is their granary, as they do not themselves cultivate the soil. This

KARA-KIRGHIZ CHINESE (MALE AND FEMALE).

country provides them flour and wheat, which they pay for with felts, skins, and sometimes with the cloth which they receive in payment for the yaks or camels which they let out to merchants. As the Wakhis are not very rich, and they sell their daughters very cheap, the Kirghiz marry them, and learn their language. From these cross-marriages are born a fair race of men, tall, with comparatively large eyes, and small men who have sometimes a long nose like the stem of a jug, not at all of the Mongol shape.

And, as we have often remarked, one need really have committed some great crime to be compelled to remain upon the Pamir, while, as a matter of fact, many of those who inhabit it have committed a murder or some other misdeed in the neighbouring countries. Compelled to fly, they come straight to the Pamir, where no one is very particular, and they spend the winter in the remote corners of the valley of Ak-Su. When the summer arrives, bringing with it the Chinese agents upon one side, and the Kunjuti upon the other, the Afghans or the Kirghiz belonging to the powerful tribes of the valley who have compromised themselves the most, make for the heights of the Alitchur, or the centre of the "roof of the world," like arkars, who live as much as they can upon inaccessible heights, out of fear of gunners, and who climb higher and higher as the snow melts at lower altitudes.

It is a motive of this kind, no doubt, an "accident" as the Corsicans put it, which has brought into the Andaman country this young man with determined features, who is not like a Kirghiz, because he is Afghan. We speak to him of Abdur-Rahman, of Ayub, of Yakoob, etc., and he knows them all. He speaks well of Yakoob, whom he will never forget, for he has broken bread with him. For his own part, his one desire is to leave this country, although he has married here and has got a child. He offers us a cup full of cream (*kaïmak*), and the comparative cleanliness of the cup would suffice to show that he is not a native of this district. His long fingers also indicate his origin, as well as his razor-shaped face. We make him a small present, and he tells us that our guide will be his father-in-law, who, he adds, is an "ichan," that is to say, a personage whose piety and honourable mode of life give him the reputation of saintliness.

The becoming manner of this Afghan, his nice way of speaking, and the gratitude which he says that he feels for his former chief, his anxiety to live elsewhere and better his condition, all go to prove his superiority over those around him, and we are not shocked at his calling us "brothers;" while we find the same pleasure in meeting him that you do when you are away from home, and get some fellow-countryman to talk to.

The man with two sheep, who also lends us three yaks, knows the ugly Satti-Kul, and would have much liked to see him to ask for the money due for four sheep sold to him some time ago. The fellow has so many debts that it is no wonder he decamped.

April 18th.

From Tchilab, we go along a path cut on the side of the rocky mountain, and leaving to our right the Bir-Kutdja (the eagle's nest), an overhanging rock with caves in which one can take shelter, we descend on to the ice of a reservoir formed by an arm of the Ak-Su, which flows westward. The watershed, at an altitude of 13,750 feet, is crossed.

We go through the snow, putting to flight wolves which do not seem very much afraid of us, and having got beyond Rabut, the site of which is marked by four mud walls, still floundering about in the melted snow, we arrive at Basaï-Gumbaz, which the Kirghiz call Basaï-Bi. It is a *mégnil* (mausoleum) of the ordinary shape—four square walls surmounted by a cone. There are a few tombs in the lower part, rectangular constructions, with a stone at each corner. At the further end is the white steep road which leads to the pass of Akjir. Our guide, the "ichan," or pir, gets off his horse and recites a prayer before the tombs. Having finished his prayer, he tells us that this monument was erected in memory of some Kirghiz killed by the Kunjuti in a fight.

"When did this occur?"

" A long time ago."

This is about the date you are given for any crime in this country, or most other parts of Asia.

The valley of Ak-Su narrows in, and brushwood is seen

peeping above the snow. The soil undergoes a change of aspect; the left bank, facing north, is white, but the right bank is steep, and one can distinguish loess, granite, red sandstone, and schist. The scenery is bright, for though the hollow places are full of snow, you can see the earth, which has shaken off her shroud as for a resurrection.

At times, we go on to the ice of the river, and at others we

VALLEY OF THE WESTERN OXUS (NORTH-EAST).

pick our way over the rocks until we halt at the bottom of a ravine in the gorge of Ak-Beles.

The south-west wind is blowing a gale, and we shave ourselves as best we can.

We discover a good many roots and stems, with which we make a flaming fire, thanks to the gusts of wind. The yaks do not come in till six o'clock. The encampment is an excellent one, with the water running below us, and a tiny stream of it trickling over the ice and snow. It is a pleasure to see the limpid stream and watch it sparkle.

So thinks Abdur-Rasul, as he sings a ballad in a loud tone of voice, the babble of the river being his accompaniment. The tall, fair Kirghiz, who is also an artist, sings in his turn a song to celebrate the exploits of a thief famous for his barantas. The melody is melancholy and monotonous, and the short phrases terminate in a modulation which sounds like a man out of breath or trying to hide a hiccough. These Andaman men live at such an altitude that one can understand their being short of breath, nor can one wonder at their songs being melancholy, for they inhabit a very melancholy country, and one cannot expect much gaiety from them.

April 19th.

We follow the right bank of the Wakhan-Darya, of the western Ak-Su (Oxus), and it is not without some difficulty and risk of breaking our necks that we scale the rocks and descend into the valley of Mirza-Murad, where we lose sight of the Ak-Su, which is hidden from our view by hills to the left.

We emerge from the spongy and boggy valley of Mirza-Murad by way of a defile which leads into the valley of Langar-Su. An enormous stone stands in the bed of the river, which our guide calls the Tchatir-tach (tent-stone); and, as a proof that it deserves this name, we find at the foot of it traces of an encampment, and a good deal of dung. Parties of travellers had sheltered themselves behind it, and had lighted fires which had left streaky black marks upon its sides. Close to it there is some grass in the broken ground of a sort of turf-bog, with snow in the hollow places and watered by intermingling streams which trickle out in large numbers from the side of the bank.

On the islets formed by the river, which are approached by numberless small bridges of snow and ice, beneath which water can be heard bubbling, there is a good deal of brushwood; more than brushwood, a regular vegetation in fact, with shrubs over six feet in height. And as everything in this world is relative, Pepin, who is very fond of forests, exclaims, "At last we can see some woods!"

We ascend the right bank, and upon the upper part of the plateau we see at least two hundred yaks, under the keeping of dogs and about ten shepherds.

We come down again to encamp in the delta of a gorge,

VALLEY OF THE WESTERN OXUS (EAST).

through which the path runs, and we send the "pir" on as ambassador. He is first to ask for milk and butter, and then to announce our presence with great care and caution. The great thing is to avoid frightening these people, and not ask anything of them, so that they may not disappoint us by making off during the night. We are on Afghan territory, the Wakhan having recently been annexed by Abdur-Rahman-Khan. We have not yet seen anything of the Afghan post, which they told us was established, if not at Ak-Beles, certainly at Langar.

The Kirghiz arrive and settle down beside our tent. The

same evening they tell us that they will not go any further, their excuse being that the yaks are exhausted. One of them was paid in advance for three days' march, and he has been only two. He, of course, does not talk of refunding the money, and wants to go back like the rest.

They have been paid in advance, and mean going off during the night, but we will keep a look-out on them. We will hobble

LANGAR.

their horses like our own, for the snow is falling, and they might stray and be devoured by wolves, or else stolen.

The pir comes back and tells us that he can see no one in the shelters inhabited by the shepherds the day before, for they are all upon the plateau. Their chief will come, for the pir has told him that we have khames, or pieces of cloth.

Over the top of the bank appears a small man, clad in sheepskins, with a rough, bushy red beard. We salute him, and ask him to draw up to the fire, but he understands neither Turkish or Persian, and the intervention of the pir is required to tell him that he can come and drink a cup of tea. He does not seem quite convinced, but he comes down and seats himself near the pir.

The new-comer has regular features, a smaller face than the Kirghiz, and light eyes, so far as can be seen through the dense eyebrows and cap drawn down so low. He wears goatskin boots. None of us can make out a word he says, though Rachmed says that his language is something like that spoken by the Yagnaous, who inhabit, to the west of the Pamir, the mountains of Kohistan.

This short, squat old man, who might almost be taken for a shepherd of the Ardennes, is soon joined by several others of different types. One is tall and slight, with a small head, a straight nose, a thick black beard, black eyes of European shape, and long hands, reminding me of certain Roumanians that I know.

They are all small and thin, with very low foreheads and delicate features, the wild bearing of wolves, but more full of nerve and muscle than the men of the Pamir.

The youngest of them, about eighteen years old, and with a perfectly smooth face, has long hair of a light red colour, which falls from under his cap on to his shoulders. He has small blue eyes, a long and straight nose, the short upper lip displaying small teeth in pretty good condition. He has a round chin, and his profile is that of a Roman—one of those who tended the flocks in the Roman campagna in the time of Hadrian. He would not have seemed out of place among the companions of Romulus and Remus.

Among these Wakhis, flat cheekbones and large eyes are the exception. We are glad to see them, for they indicate the vicinity of the Hindu-Kush, and of India.

I pass over the interminable discussion, interlarded by threats, promises, gestures, and worse, which went on for two days before we could get the Wakhis to provide us with the yaks we required, and all this in five different languages. It was like the tower of Babel.

You need a strong dose of patience to traffic with the Wakhis, or the Pamir Kirghiz; and the early Greeks would be as well able to drive a bargain with the men of Gascony, or the Carthaginians with the original inhabitants of Marseilles.

At last the bargain is struck, and they agree to convey our baggage in the direction of the Kunjut, by way of the Tash-Kupruk, and we pay them in advance for three days' march, half in silver bars, half in cloth. At first, I thought that we should not succeed in coming to terms, for they had moved away their herds of yaks, and had prepared apparently for a start. But, thanks to the pir, who speaks their language very well, and who inspires them with confidence, they became tamer; and then the Kirghiz of Andaman, whom we had hired, had made a vain attempt to fly during the night. We kept a sharp look-out on them by day, and gave them distinct notice that we should shoot them down at the first attempt they made to escape. We added, that the only way in which they could regain their liberty, as they would not go any further, was to induce the Wakhis to take their place. They soon saw that we were in earnest, and, finding this to be the case, they at once accepted the proposal we made them of winning over the Wakhis. It was really curious to watch the faces of the Kirghiz as as they sang our praises, and declared that they would go to the end of the world with us if they had better animals, and were not obliged to go and fetch flour for their famishing families.

According to both Kirghiz and Wakhis, three days' march will suffice to bring us to the frontier of the Kunjut. Then we shall have to go over a pass, and in three days more we shall be at Miskar, a village where we shall find an abundance of everything.

As soon as the Kirghiz are paid off, we start, despite the snow and the lateness of the hour, it being past one when we begin to climb the left bank of the Langar-Su. By a rapid descent on the other side, we reach the valley of the Ak-Su, and at this very moment the snow stops, the sky is azure blue, and the sun quite warm. At our feet, the new grass is just shooting out of the earth, and our horses cannot resist the temptation of nibbling at it. If we let them have their way, they would not go any further.

THE VALLEY OF TASH-KUPRUK.

It is so hot that we roll up our cloaks and tie them on to the saddle-bow, and we remark with pleasure the presence of tall willows in the valley, some of them fully eighteen feet high; our road taking us through quite a forest of wild rose bushes.

Crossing the river several times, we halt at Beikara, near some huts made of dry stone, our course having been first east, and then south-east. We can just distinguish the point at which the valley narrows, about an hour away, and it is at this point that it takes the name of Tash-Kupruk and that the snow begins again, for everything is quite white.

From Beïkara, we arrived, in an hour, at the gorge from which the Siah-Ab (black water) of the Wakhis takes its source. It is impossible to cross it, there being places where a horse could not swim over. Upon the right bank, the route is broken at several places by deep crevices and ravines, and though the left bank is not so steep, there is much more snow. Though melting, it was still over six feet deep, and I really do not know how we got through it. It took us more than six hours to reach the Tash-

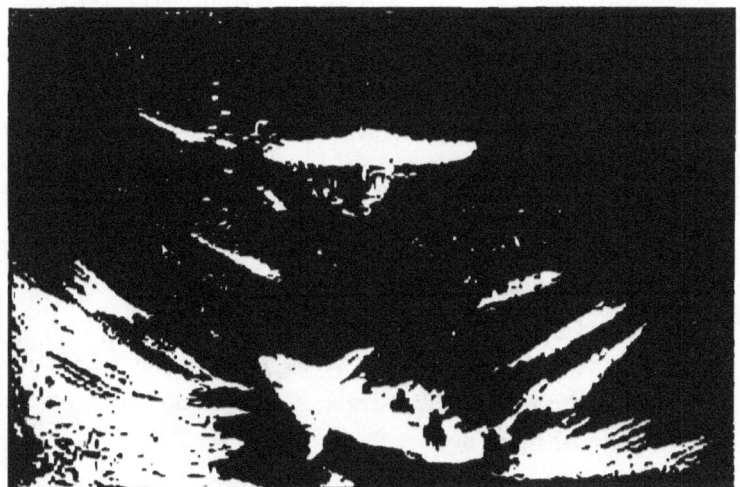

TASH-KUPRUK.

Kupruk, with its bridge of stones, which is very solid and which owes nothing to the hand of man. An enormous block of stone, which had rolled down from above, had fallen right into the crevice, and been caught there, as in a cleft stick, where it has remained, and now forms a bridge, beneath which the dark waters of the Siah-Ab seethe and roar, attempting to force a broader passage for themselves.

The day has been a very severe one; the men are worn out,

. and the Wakhis, as well as the single Kirghiz who has accompanied us with a yak, seem very dissatisfied.

The night is a splendid one, the three stars which form the Balance (Tarasun) shining just on the sky-line of the mountain, Venus being as it were a picturesque dot to the *i* represented by a peak over which she was visible.

April 22nd.

The remaining Kirghiz made off during the night. The Wakhis refuse to go any further, and we have to beat them, as promises are of no avail. One of them has laid down, and has declared that he will kill himself if we touch him. This is the first allusion I have heard to suicide in this part of the world. Finding that we do not give way to them, they make up their minds to go on, after loading the pir with curses for getting them into such a mess. The pir says nothing in reply, and goes on in advance to look for a path.

We do not get more than four miles or so in over ten hours, the men being obliged to carry the baggage on their backs the best part of the way. The marvel is that we do not break our necks a hundred times over.

At 7 p.m., we encamp upon a spur where there is some tchibaque, a grass of which the horses are very fond, and which is also used for fuel, while close by we have some willows as thick round as your arm. We march towards the south-east, now along the crest, now descending into the bed of a torrent, now hacking steps for the horses to put their feet into over the ice which covers the smooth snow. In order to get a horse over, one man holds him by the rope—not by the bridle, as that would interfere with his movements—a second by the tail, and a third by his stirrups or pack-saddle, while a fourth helps to steady him, steadying himself with his stick. The yaks go on alone, being extraordinarily sure-footed.

YADIK HAS A FALL.

It is not very cold, for at nine this morning there are only sixteen degrees of frost, while at the same hour in the evening there are only nine.

April 23rd.

Our first thought, on waking, is as to the Wakhis, and as to whether they have made off during the night. We were not much afraid of it, for they were quite done up, and, wild as they are, they could not well travel by night the road which they had so much difficulty in getting over by day.

Upon the contrary, this morning they are very pliable, and are quite willing to go another day, if we will pay them in advance, which we do.

We continue to follow the right bank, amid the jagged fragments of rock, making the best progress we can. The left bank is still very steep.

We descend into a ravine, ascend again to the crest, our horses falling and picking themselves up again. Every now and then, we see some wild goats, with a wolf on the watch for them. Fall succeeds fall, and the heat gets so great, that at 4 p.m. there are eighty-five degrees, while at 8 a.m. there had been sixteen degrees of frost. The yaks begin to pant and show symptoms of viciousness.

While trying to hold up a horse which was slipping slowly back, Sadik himself slips and glides down to the bottom like a thunderbolt, rolling over and over three or four times, and being stopped only by the accumulated snow at the bottom. He does not hurt himself in the least, and picks himself up with a laugh. The pir, who is looking on, laughs and says in a very funny way, "Avoua, Sadik! Avoua, Sadik!"

These are about the only comic incidents we have.

At last we arrive at some stony and round hills, and we encamp at Bala-Guizine, at the foot of a gorge descending from the east. To the south, we have some peaks of snowy whiteness, like a bridal veil, and then our course is towards the south-east.

The provision of bread we laid in at Osch is exhausted, having lasted just fifty days, and Sadik makes some large cakes to last several days. Beasts and men alike are worn out with fatigue, and the Wakhis manifest their intention of turning back.

CROSSING THE BALA-GUIZINE.

April 24th.

We advance in a south-west direction, passing over the ice, and the valley opens out, being no more than a gorge when within an hour's march of Bala-Guizine.

We have a daran, or a very easy sort of pass, in front of us, but this pass proves to be deceptive, as when we have got over it, we find ourselves back in the same valley. In front of us is a ravine which stops the progress of the horses, and it is not without some difficulty that we hit upon a means of getting them across.

Towards evening, the pir and Sadik, whom we had sent on to reconnoitre, return and tell us that the valley ends in a *cul-de-sac*, where the snow has accumulated in such quantities that we shall never get over it. This is a very serious matter, for the animals are quite exhausted, and so, too, are the men. I must go and see to-morrow, and perhaps we shall have to decide upon retracing our steps. We encamp at a place which the pir calls Zarsotte.

The Wakhis have shown a lot of temper all day, and our meat is beginning to go bad, our staple food being *terek* (millet).

April 25th.

Snow fell during the night. The north-west wind is blowing a hurricane. The Wakhis have made off during the night, taking their yaks with them and leaving two dogs behind. We send Abdur-Rasul and Menas after them; but they soon return, and report that the Wakhis have five or six hours' start and cannot be overtaken.

The pir, Rachmed, and myself go to reconnoitre the road in the direction of the Kunjut. If we cannot possibly get through, we shall leave our baggage at Zarsotte with Menas, to whom we shall give a week's provision of millet-flour and one horse. We shall go on to Langar and see what can be done towards securing provisions and beasts of burden. If a caravan comes by we shall borrow from it what we require, or, in the event of refusal, take it by force, paying a fair price for it.

If we succeed in getting through, we shall leave our baggage behind, to shift for itself, go on foot to the Kunjut and get together carriers and yaks who will return to Zarsotte and fetch the baggage. If things turn out badly, we shall have no further need for baggage.

We take the indispensable tools with us—an axe to cut out the ice, a pickaxe, a wooden shovel, two horses, and a few handfuls of barley for them, and so we start, staff in hand.

Following alternately the ice along the banks, or the ridge of the overhanging hills, we march for three hours and a half to a point where two streams meet and form the river. One comes down from the north-east through a very narrow valley which becomes a mere gorge, the other from the south-east.

We arrive, by a steep ascent and with six feet of snow in places, at a hill which divides the two gorges, near which are columns about thirty-three feet high, with blocks of stone upon their tops; a very curious phenomenon of erosion. Upon the top we find the snow so deep that the horses cannot get through it. We take them to a sheltered spot where they will find a little grass, and we go on our route, or rather pick it out as we proceed. It is impossible to venture below, as the snow is too deep, except upon the very edge of the precipice, and we climb on to a sort of table-land, with pieces of rock dotted all over it, but here, again, the route is an impracticable one. We are on the left bank of the river which comes down from the south-east, and we remark that on the right bank there is but little snow. The question is, however, how to get there, for we cannot fly over the gorge, in the bottom of which we can see the water through the holes in the ice.

A little higher up we can see the wrinkles of a glacier between the steep sides of a rock coming down sheer. That is where the pass will be found, according to the pir, and it makes a bend E.S.E., as far as can be judged by the snow, which begins to fall. The pir, who is as light in his movements as a bird, goes on in front, and, halting for a moment on the edge of a rock, he turns round, and says to us—

"I shall go on as long as my strength lasts. If I do not come back, you will know that the road is good. Put a little bread in my bag and leave it where the horses are. Put my cloak under cover, so that the wind will not blow it away."

Rachmed just manages to reach the pir, giving him some apricots and a little bread, and he comes back with the cloak, which the worthy fellow has thrown off so as to be able to walk better in the snow. The pir is soon out of sight, and the snow-flakes get thicker and the wind higher. The indefatigable walker then reappears on the other side of the gorge, and we watch him falling in the snow, getting up again, and finally disappearing for good. The wind blows more fiercely until it has reached a perfect

UPON THE ROAD TO THE KUNJUT.

hurricane, and Rachmed is persuaded that we shall never see the pir again, that he is buried in the snow, and that he is lost. He mutters a prayer over him, in which we can just make out the words Allah and Mahomet, and as we sit crouching in our cloaks from the storm, we fervently hope that the plucky old man has not come to any harm.

At five o'clock, seeing no signs of him, we determine to retrace our steps, and the wind is so strong that it prevents us from breathing or hearing. At last we get to our horses, give them the last few handfuls of barley, mixed with a little grass which we had cut at the encampment and put into a bag, and retrace our steps, Rachmed calling out every few minutes in Kirghiz fashion, "Pir O-ó-ó! Pir O-ó-ó!" As soon as we get to the valley of Zarsotte, we have the wind straight in our teeth, and we cannot go ten paces without stopping to turn our backs to it and catch breath. We are almost suffocated, and quite exhausted. Upon the crest of the hill we put up some "emperor partridges," as they are named in Turkestan, and we can hear them calling. Whereupon Rachmed remarks, "Those birds are stronger than we are; they have not lost their voice."

At several places we have to cut out steps for our horses and ourselves. The ice has got in under our boots, and we slip about as we go on. It is, in truth, a most trying wind.

At nightfall, the plucky pir comes up with us, and we make him wrap a good cloak around his body, for he is very hot. He tells us that we cannot get over the snow, as it is melting, and will not bear us. He thought several times that he should never extricate himself; but, by God's help, he had succeeded in doing so. He had seen no sign of any path for beasts of burden, and according to him it is either too late or too soon to get through. It will be best, he says, to wait till the snow melts.

We reach the end of our stage at 9 p.m., all three very tired. The tempest lasts all night, and having secured the tent-pegs, we go off to sleep convinced that we must give up the Kunjut. To-morrow we shall start for Langar.

After having destroyed the objects which were not strictly indispensable, keeping only three canteens, the provisions, and the bedding, we start for Langar on the 26th of April. Menas remains with the canteens, and he will have to sustain himself on flour and millet. For the last three days we have had neither meat nor salt. As the salted fish forms part of our reserve with the smoked meat, we shall not touch it until all the flour is eaten and we cannot possibly get any more provisions. In the meanwhile, we eat some flour mixed with fat.

In the evening of the 28th, we reach Langar, where we see no signs of any smoke, nor a single yak. The Wakhis have taken to their heels.

On the way, we found the dead bodies of the horses which we had abandoned on the way, and the wolves had eaten two, while close to a third we saw traces of an animal like a panther. We lost two more horses, that of Pepin breaking its back. Pepin then put a bullet through its head, and Rachmed partially skinned it, so as to have some leather to make us slippers, such as are worn in his country.

While we are putting up our tent, we send the pir, Sadik, and Rachmed to reconnoitre. The pir will endeavour to get the Wakhis back by persuasion; while the two others will use money or force, as they think best. But they return without having been able to catch a sight of the fugitives.

Early to-morrow morning, the pir will start for Andaman, and endeavour to bring back the Kirghiz, with some yaks; in any case, he will bring us the carcases of two sheep and a little salt, if he can find any. We shall wait for his return, stopping the first caravan that comes this way.

April 29th.

The snow is still falling, with a strong westerly wind. While we are resting in our tent, the dogs begin to bark, and Abdur-Rasul declares that he can see a camel on the top of the ridge. I tell Rachmed to take his revolver and sword, and go and see what it all means, enjoining upon him to say, if the caravan is one of traders, that we want to buy some *khames* (Kashgar cloth). He soon comes back, falling rather than walking down the hill, in order to tell us with breathless haste—

"It is the Afghan Abdullah-Khan, whom Allah has sent to us. He is coming to see us."

It is wonderful how everything has fitted in nicely during our journey. Had we arrived a day later at Langar, Abdullah-Khan would have been gone. And then to what a pass we should have been brought! For Abdullah-Khan, who comes up a few minutes after Rachmed, gave us information which shows us that the pir will fail to bring back any Kirghiz or yaks.

After having said his prayer, broken bread, and drunk the cup of tea we are still able to offer him, the Afghan says—

"As soon as you had left Ak-Tach, the Kirghiz met and held council. They were anxious to attack you, kill you, and strip you of all you possessed. They thought to be making themselves agreeable to the Chinese, and to be ensuring a good booty; they were all agreed as to that, but when it came to the ways and means, there was a great difference of opinion. The young men were full of ardour; but an old man who had seen your arms made very sensible objections to this course, saying, 'These men have formidable weapons; they are upon their guard, and we must not attack them openly, or by day. At night, they will perhaps hear you, and will at once fire. It is an easy matter to seize their horses, but they will come back to fetch them, and you will be obliged to fight. They are *bahadours* (brave men), and before you have killed them all, they will have done for more than one of you. Am I not right.' They said that he was, and so the project for attacking you was abandoned.

"The same day that it was known at Ak-Tach that you had left Kizil-Khorum and that you must be at the source of the Oxus or upon Afghan territory, two pig-tailed Chinese, representatives of the daotaï, arrived with an armed escort of horsemen. They called together the bis and reproached them with having let you pass; but the latter excused themselves upon the ground

ENCAMPMENT BEYOND BALA-GULINE.

of your having many large and small guns, which contain innumerable cartridges, and that you had only passed through the district. The Chinese then sent for the Kirghiz of Andaman, who had assisted you, but they did not come. At first, the Chinese were inclined to go in pursuit of you, but they were told that you were already on Afghan territory, and that the Emir of Cabul would be dissatisfied if his frontier was violated. So they remained at Ak-Tach. There then came a great chief, who sent letters, with an order for horsemen to be despatched

HORNLESS YAK AND CAMEL OF THE PAMIR.

from Tashkurgan. He took down the names of those who helped you and intends to punish them.

"As I came along, I saw the dead bodies of the horses you had abandoned, and I learned that Sarik-Mahmed had taken to flight as soon as he heard of the Chinese being on the way."

We asked Abdullah if he has met the pir, and he says no, but he is sure the pir had seen him and concealed himself.

We tell him what our position is, and ask him if he cannot lend us some of his animals to go and fetch our baggage and Menas. We shall like to conclude the bargain to-day, so that to-morrow the yaks may start for Tash-Kupruk.

He says that as he is intending to discharge the Kirghiz, who take advantage of him, this can be easily arranged, and he undertakes to have our baggage taken to Sarhad, whither he will despatch a man on foot to fetch beasts and carriers, so that we may start together.

We at once send Menas and Sadik to the Kirghiz, with Abdullah-Khan, and, after an interminable discussion, the Kirghiz agree to go to Tash-Kupruk with five yaks, on condition that they are paid £4 for each yak. It is useless telling them that two yaks will be enough, and we have to submit to their terms.

They take the three extra yaks, because they want to fetch some willow wood for their tents, and they know that they are masters of the situation and can make us pay well for "the pleasure of being useful to those whom they like so well." Such is the answer I get from a rascal whom I ask why he bleeds us so. He adds that if we were not who we are, their price would be much higher. How kind!

They go off with Sadik on the 30th of April, and we wait for them until the 3rd of May, passing our time talking, watching the snow fall, and digesting our "tchousma," that is to say, the porridge made of flour cooked in fat, for which we have not, unfortunately, any salt. Our stomachs feel the want of it, and our gums are very sore.

May 3rd.

The barking of our dogs tells us that we may expect a visitor, and up comes the pir on foot, leading his horse. The worthy fellow drops rather than sits down by the fire.

He gets a hearty welcome from us all, and we unload his horse, which is a mere bag of bones. From one bag, we take two sheep cut up into joints, and a small leathern bottle containing sour milk, while the pir produces half a pound of salt from his waistband. He then explains why he has not got any yaks.

"As soon as the Kirghiz heard of my return, they assembled in large numbers outside my tent. Some of them wanted to know what had become of you, while others, whom fear of the Chinese had made vindictive, wanted to maltreat me. The old bi whom you saw at Mulkali, bitterly upbraided me for having shown you the way, and he told his men to tie my hands and feet, put me on to a yak, and hand me over to the Chinese. I told him that I was Nur-Djane the *divana* (dervish), that it was my duty to lend aid to any one who asked me for it, and that in labouring for you, I was labouring for Allah.

"One man exclaimed angrily that I had received money from you, and that I had betrayed them, and cared more for you than for them. I replied that I had never asked for any pay from the Feringhis, and that what they gave me I had accepted for the sake of my children. I had several people on my side. My son-in-law came up; he is an Afghan, as you know, and he took my part courageously, whereupon my enemies, seeing that they were the weaker, withdrew. We killed two of my sheep, and here I am with them. You will let me go back at once, for the Chinese are close at hand, my horses are very poor, my cattle are weak, and it will perhaps be difficult for me to get away. The position is a very awkward one, the Chinese are cruel, and my presence among my own people is indispensable. I am in a hurry to get away. By God's help, all difficulties will be got over."

We give him the present he has so well earned, and Rachmed has a little meat cooked for him, while Abdur-Rasul pours him out a cup of tea. He eats as fast as his almost toothless jaws will permit; gets up, tightens his belt, puts his bag upon his horse, and, coming close up to us after listening to our thanks with an unconcerned air, raises his hand to his beard and exclaims, "Allah is great!" Our men shake hands with him, and he bestrides his horse and makes off.

At the same moment, some yaks make their appearance upon the opposite bank, and we soon see Menas scuttling down the incline with all speed, and he falls like a famished man upon the bowl of sour milk presented to him by his friend Rachmed, and between two pulls at it, he tells us that he has got on very well, that he has brought back a horse which we had abandoned, that his own has fallen into a precipice, and that he has been obliged to kill it. He is very pleased to see us again. He asks about the pir, and we point out to him the latter, who is riding off with his

THE PIR.

legs dangling from his horse, which he is doing his best to urge into a feeble trot. Menas shouts to wish him good-bye, and the pir turns round to wave his hand to him and soon disappears behind the Tchatir-Tach (stone-tent).

What a curious physiognomy is his among such a collection of ruffians! What an ugly but honest face he has! We shall long remember his head, shaped like a top, broad at the top, with bulging forehead and prominent cheekbones, narrow at the lower end, with sunken cheeks and small square chin, and the tiny grey eyes which glitter with such an air of shrewdness in their deep orbits, and his narrow nose, like the beak of a bird of prey, bent down towards his pursed-up mouth. How he walks, too, for a man of over sixty, and with what a light step! Where we sink into the snow, he seems to glide over it. He is not troubled with superfluous flesh, for though he is of a fair height, he does not weigh eight stone.

He never asked for a piece of bread, never asked to come near the fire, never proffered a complaint. The fact is that Nur-Djane had many youthful misdeeds to atone for. He had not always had the fear of God before his eyes. He is credited with having committed every species of crime, with endless raids (*barantas*), and with having been the terror of the Pamir. He appeared and disappeared as if by enchantment, being as intangible as the wind. His revenges were terrible, and his threats were never made in vain. In short, if rumour is to be believed, Nur-Djane must have been the greatest of criminals until the date of his startling conversion.

This occurred twenty years ago, and followed upon a dream, during which he saw himself in a swollen river, being beaten about by the torrent. When he tried to swim to the bank, the raging waters drove him down to the bottom of the abyss, and each time that he rose to the surface, he seemed to be further from shore. For a long time, he was tossed about in this way, and when the banks had faded out of sight, he felt himself hopelessly lost, for the torrent had opened out into a raging sea, the waves were mighty, and the night was dark.

Nur-Djane regarded this dream as a warning from heaven, and he determined to spend the rest of his days in doing good. He said the five prayers regularly, took up the staff of the dervish, and went off to Khojend, where he sought the counsel of famous mollahs and illustrious "pirs." He goes to Khojend every year to listen to extracts from holy books. The people of the Pamir, of the Alaï, and of the Wakhan know him, and he acts as their go-between when they are at variance, conveying proposals from one aoul to another, praying at the bedside of the new-born babe and of the dead. He is universally respected, for his sole thought is to do good. And he is called Nur-Djane-Divana, the dervish, the lunatic, as so much kindness of heart can only be the mark of a disordered brain. Others call him Nur-Djane-Kalifa, the caliph, this being an honourable epithet. In the eyes of the great majority, he is a saint. So he is in ours, and my readers will probably be of the same opinion.

We never caught him in a lie, for he always kept his word, and helped his companions to the utmost of his power.

When I arrived with him close to Langar, we were rejoined by the Kirghiz. One of them asked him if we had a letter from the daotaï, that he dared to show us the way without an order from Kashgar. He replied at once that he had not, and when the Kirghiz said that he was risking his life, he replied, " I am not afraid of the Chinese, I am only afraid of doing what is wrong. Allah!"

One meets with honest people everywhere, but not with many, and that is why I have spoken at some length of this one.

AHMED.

ENCAMPMENT NEAR LANGAR.

CHAPTER XV.

STOPPED IN THE TCHATRAL.

We start for the Wakhan—Carthaginian traders—Sadik and Abdur-Rasul leaves us—The Afghans try to detain us at Sarhad—We cross the Hindu-Kush without a guide—Meeting the Tchatralis—This time we are stopped—Our resources exhausted—The Tchatralis—Negotiations—The Anglo-Indian Government intervenes—Forty-nine days at Mastudj—We are released—Hayward—Speedy return.

THE men and beasts of burden that Abdullah-Khan has asked for have arrived from Sarhad at Langar. We are about to start for the Afghan frontier, we shall reach the pass of Baroguil and enter the Tchatral. If possible, we shall go by the glacier of Darcot, in order to reach first Yassin and then Kashmir. We hope that we have seen the last of the snow, and the thought that, further on, we shall find wood, water, and a warm climate, gives us good heart. We pay little heed to the men we may meet, for we are determined not to flinch; while those we may encounter will be astonished to see us arrive, as was the case with the men of the Pamir, and we shall hurry through their midst, just as wolves, with their coats bristling and their fangs displayed, make their way through a pack of hounds.

We have conveyed our baggage on the horses of the Wakhis to the encampment of Abdullah-Khan, which is pitched at the entrance to a gorge. This encampment is very animated, and the fires are visible above the bushes, where the swarm of Wakhis is clustered below us; horses and yaks being tethered in such a way that they can browse on the grass around the encampment. These people, with a European cast of countenance and dressed in frieze, are very talkative and noisy. They are preparing to start to-morrow, and we have not heard any noise for so long that their uproar is quite a pleasant sensation to us.

We are naturally the object of much curiosity upon the part of these natives, who are under the escort of tall old men, with white beards and long robes; these chiefs, with their judicial air, as if they were the most dignified of men, are about the most cunning. It is extraordinary how deceitful they are; oaths fall from their mouths as readily as good morning, and five minutes afterwards they boldly deny what they had said five minutes before, when invoking the names of God and of the Prophet. They play the most contradictory parts, passing without transition from tragic to comic, from comic to pathetic. Around the greybeards are some fifty individuals howling, gesticulating and chattering. One of them joins in the conversation, apostrophizing the speaker, reproaching him with sacrificing the interests of his own people, with not thinking of the families to be fed, the difficulties of the route, and so forth. Every kind of falsehood, in fact, was put forward with the utmost coolness, in order to make us pay more dearly for their services, and perhaps in part as a mere pastime. The opportunity was a favourable one for unloosing their tongues after the long winter's sleep, and so they talk like the heroes of Homer. They have a gifted imagination, and are not chary of their words.

Add to this that they are not blind to their interests, and knowing the Afghans as well as the Feringhis to be at their mercy, they shear them very close.

Amid all these excitable people, Abdullah-Khan, seated upon his heels, is as calm as a martyr exposed to the insults of a furious populace. He replies to all of them in the same tranquil manner, rarely losing his temper, refuting all their arguments, and this for hours together. He only resolves to withdraw when his adversaries cut short all discussion by exorbitant demands, and begin to quarrel among themselves. He then gets up, comes towards us and says, "They are savages. What is the use of trying to do anything," with a shrug of the shoulders.

The only companion of Abdullah-Khan, a man named Achmet-Khan, is of quite a different temperament. He does not seem born for debate, and he avoids it altogether, leaving it to his friend to try and persuade the Wakhis. While all this talk is going on, he holds aloof, remaining leaning on his bales, with his cap pulled down over his eyes. His eyes glitter, his hooked nose dilates, he shakes his broad shoulders, shows his white teeth in his access of temper, and, with his lips constantly moving, mutters insults and threats in his own tongue. He, at all events, regrets not being the master, and if he had the Wakhis at his mercy, he would make them smart. He strikes me as being the type of the primitive traders of antiquity, the pushing Carthaginians; of those who made the circuit of Africa, or plunged into the deserts, compelling men, with the point of their swords, to buy their goods. While leading a life of this kind, they learnt the art of struggling with men, as well as the art of persuading them, and there were no limits to their audacity. Having often been at the mercy of their savage customers, who sometimes plundered them without mercy, they were in turn merciless, when they could be so without detriment to their interests. Carrying back to their country the qualities developed by their traffic with barbarians, they made use of them for directing the course of public affairs, and sometimes compromised their fellow-countrymen, but the habit of making a profit, and their anxiety about the strong box, prevented them

WAKHIS.

from anything like far-seeing views and paralyzed their energies, whereas the Romans had higher views or less paltry ways.

I had forgotten to mention that Sadik and Abdur-Rasul left us on the 3rd of May; taking with them on horseback millet and flour, with bread enough to last several days. They cut some enormous sticks, which are better than a sword in their hands.

We are somewhat anxious about them, as they will find it no easy matter to get safe through the Pamir.

Sadik had at one time some little difficulty with the Wakhis, and this is a good reason why he should not return home by the Wakhan and the Badakshan. These two men have served us loyally and well, and their conduct is above all praise.*

In the afternoon of May 4th, after a discussion which has been going on since sunrise, the Wakhis load the goods and merchandise and make a start, and we reach Sarhad on the afternoon of May 7th, snow falling and melting as it fell.

The route we followed is a delightful one, by comparison with the Pamir and Tash-Kupruk. Yet many a traveller would regard it as a terrible one, for it is all up and down hill, while some of the paths, winding from rock to rock, are no wider than one's hand, with a sheer precipice on one side. But the heights have an air of life given to them by the willows, the birch-trees and the junipers, the last time that we saw any of these latter having been at Ak-Basoga, in the Ferghana. Sparrows with very bright plumage were singing in the branches. We then crossed the Wakhan-Darya, or western Ak-Su, twelve times, and nothing could have been more picturesque than the crossing of the ferry, with the yaks swimming, and the naked men urging them on; while we got a very pleasant and fresh bath. We were first on the right and then on the left bank, and as the valley narrowed into a gorge we made our way to the summit. The weather was fine on the 4th, but snow fell on the other days. We had, however, plenty of wood.

The Afghans and the Wakhis were at loggerheads every day, the latter refusing to go any further, and in the end they obtained a few extra *karbasses* (pieces of cloth). Even Abdullah-Khan at

* Sadik and Abdur-Rasul were stopped by the Chinese Kirghiz, and it was not until the end of July, after they had been stripped of everything, that they reached the first tents of the Ferghana.

last got out of temper with them, and as to Achmet-Khan, he would have killed them if he could have had his way.

We did not come upon any villages, and our encampments are at Sang-Kuk, Iochkh, upon the edge of a torrent.

Before coming to Sarhad, the valley of Wakhan-Darya gets broader, the mountain undulates as if the plain was close, and we find a good road over the hills, though, in order to make a short cut, we come down the sides, our horses slipping so much that we get off and follow the bed of the river on foot, only remounting them to get over any deep pool of water.

The Wakhis, who speak Persian, are much amused when I tell them that the fifty pieces of cloth which they had wrung out of us this morning had shortened the route by a day. They swore by Allah and Mahomet that it would take two days' march to go from the last encampment to Sarhad. They then point to a small plain, which to us looks like a mere blotch upon the horizon, and say that this is Sarhad.

As we proceed, we see stone cottages like those of the Kohistan, with square walls, flat roofs, and cattle lairs in the courtyards, many women, dark and thin, with regular and rather fine features, being seated in front of the doors. The air is filled with the hum and stir of village life, with the crying of children, the lowing of cattle, and the barking of dogs. Here and there are square bits of cultivated land, surrounded by brushwood which formed a fence. Narrow channels are cut for irrigation. The few houses to be met with are built up against a rock, which thus serves not only as a wall but as a roof.

The stones are very dark in colour, and the soil quite black, and as the inhabitants wear grey frieze, they are not easily to be picked out, so that from a distance the houses seem to be abandoned. Those which stand upon a hill, with their sharp angles, look like so many fortresses in the snow. A few

AT SARHAD.

white willows above intercept the light, and render the picture less sombre. There are but few patches of snow about.

We encamp in a moist meadow, where the grass, green and fresh, is a great treat for our horses. We have eight horses left, and they will stand a lot of work if we give them plenty of barley. The Wakhis sell it to us at an exorbitant price, a horse costing eight shillings a day to feed.

We are very pleased to be at Sarhad, to the south of which we see the mountains opening upon the left bank of the Wakhan-Darya. This road leads to the Baraguil, and upon the other side the waters flow down into India. As the proverb has it, "Hindustan Gulistan, Turkestan Guristan;" "Hindustan is a flower-bed, Turkestan is a cemetery."

WAKHIS.

If the snow ceased falling, we should be in the grass-land of Sarhad. There is good water in the marsh, and plenty of capital snipe.

Abdullah-Khan comes to encamp near us. Achmet-Khan will arrive to-morrow with the rest of the baggage. The yaks have fallen into the water, and it has been necessary to pull out their loads, and the Wakhis refuse to go any further till they are paid extra for this.

Upon the 8th of May, when we wake up, we find a little snow falling, and it melts very fast. There is not much frost, though we are at an altitude of over ten thousand feet. At ten o'clock, the thermometer marks forty-one degrees, and it seems as if spring had come.

The reader may say to himself that we are now at the end of our troubles, that, after we and our horses are nicely rested, we shall be able quietly to cross the Hindu-Kush, and as quietly to descend into the Hindustan-Gulistan. But this is not to be. Rachmed comes to tell us that there is an Indian chief in this village, and that this chief, a *dahbachi* (chief of ten), has sent for him to cross-examine him. We forbid Rachmed to go, and tell the messenger to inform his chief that he must come and see us.

We find him to be a very small man, wearing the Afghan uniform, and followed by an escort armed with an enormous musket, the old men of Sarhad also accompanying them. After the customary greetings, we ask the dahbachi to seat himself upon a strip of felt laid down in front of our tent, and Abdullah-Khan sits down beside him. Then comes a string of questions as to where we are going and what we are doing. The conversation takes place in Persian, and as Rachmed acts interpreter, I have plenty of time to think what I shall reply. We appear to satisfy the dahbachi, who shows his sense of approval in a very dignified manner. We explain to him that we have found the passes of Akdjir and Tash-Kupruk closed, and that we have been obliged to come to Sarhad, whence we shall go to the Tchatral by way of the Baraguil.

He says that he is at our service, that we may ask for anything we require, and that he will take steps to see that nothing is left undone. We are at once to be supplied with provisions, horses, yaks, and a guide. The chief smokes his ghalyan, and slowly sips his tea, his sword dangling upon his knee in a very warlike attitude. He is a handsome young man, with a hooked nose, blue eyes, with a ring of antimony round them, and the long Afghan head. After drinking a cup of tea, he gets up and repeats that he is our slave, then going off.

Of course, they send us nothing, and when we seek to lay in a stock of provisions, they refuse to sell us any. The inhabitants have been expressly forbidden to supply us with anything. A courier is sent to Kila-Pandj to ask for reinforcements, the idea being to make us wait and eventually compel us to turn back when the soldiers have arrived.

Achmet-Khan advises us to start, but the advice is useless, as we know what to think about the Afghans. We do not want a repetition of Chour-Tepe. We will let our horses rest, purchase flour at any price, secretly, during the night, and when we have got enough to last us a week, we shall make a start, doing without a guide.

We get rid of all superfluous objects, and give a few extra feeds to two of our horses which will carry the chests. We only retain a quarter of a load for each of the other horses, and we keep upon our guard. Abdullah-Khan and Achmet do not venture to compromise themselves, for they fear being punished. They have been told that we are the same people who have been arrested at Chour-Tepe, though we repudiated all knowledge of these persons. The emir has to be considered, so they have to be very circumspect.

We wait until the 11th of May for orders from Kila-Pandj, which the dahbachi said that he must have before he could act, though in reality we have been waiting for our horses to gain a little strength. We have flour enough to last us a week, which will be as much as we shall require. Abdullah-Khan has explained to us what road we must take, saying, "You will go straight on. You will turn to the right, then take the path to the left, and afterwards look for the way."

We start at twelve precisely, and do not see a single Wakhi. The Afghan merchants help us to load our horses, and when all is ready, the tent is struck and rolled up, and on we go. The dahbachi comes and begs us to wait, but we will not listen to a word he says.

Abdullah-Khan accompanies us as far as the ferry, which

we cross on the back of a horse, which comes and goes till we are all over. We say a last good-bye to our friends, and off we go.

We marched on for six days before reaching the first village of the Tchatral. The first day the road was good, the valley rising first to the south and then to the south-west.

Upon the second day, the valley began to narrow, our course being still south-west, along paths on the sides of the rocks.

CEMETERY AND HOUSES AT SARHAD.

The snow begins falling again, and we have to feel our way through the deep snow which lies in the pass. At the same time I see some wolves, which fly at our approach. Finally we reach the watershed, at an altitude of about twelve thousand feet. I shout out the good news to those who are following behind, and we descend a little way and encamp upon a shoulder of the mountain, which is clear of snow and of quagmires.

The third day, we mistake our road, having taken the right bank of the Arkhun, which flows from east to west, and we come against a solid mass of rock, so that we are obliged to retrace our steps.

The fourth day we wade across the Arkhun, and pass by a magnificent glacier. Again crossing the Arkhun, and following the same circle which the river describes over hills covered with juniper-trees, we again come out upon the valley, which is half a mile broad, at a point where the river breaks up into several branches. This might be termed the valley of glaciers, for we can see three all at once.

Having crossed the various arms of the river several times, we encamp in a small wood, where we find plenty of grass for our horses and wood for our fires. There is also an abundance of good water, of which we drink freely, for our flour without salt is very unappetizing. We are all as poor as scarecrows, besides being dirty and in rags, with scarcely a sole to our boots. Pepin and Menas are very sick, and all the others except myself complain of nausea and pains in the stomach.

Our encampment is a charming one, and we can hear a mosquito, the first for a long time. A caterpillar falls on my face, so this is real summer at last. Yet yesterday it was still freezing, and at 11 p.m. the thermometer was several degrees below freezing point.

Upon the fifth day, after having counted seven glaciers and crossed the river seven or eight times, we take a path on the right bank which brings us to a virgin forest, where we encamp. The wind is blowing very strong, and the branches of the trees rustle and sway about so much that we half expect to hear a weathercock creak upon the roof of our next-door neighbour.

We have only enough flour to last one day, and that is bad, but no doubt we shall reach a village to-morrow, for yesterday we saw the print of a naked foot on the sand in the river bed. Going on in advance to reconnoitre, I saw some traces of a recent bivouac, and the natives have been to cut wood in the forest. They have been squaring some beams for their dwellings, and we wake upon the sixth day with the pleasant feeling that we are about to see human beings again. All nature smiles, and the weather is delightful. So we start in good spirits.

After going a little way, I hear shouts, and can distinguish the forms of men among the stones some way below. One of them jumps down from a rock, followed by a boy, and with a gun upon his shoulder. He calls out to me, but I go on as if I had not heard him. He then comes up to meet me, and he is a curious specimen of humanity, being of middle height, with a Tzigane head, a dyed beard, black eyes made to appear larger by the use of antimony, long hair gathered up into a Neapolitan fisherman's cap made of grey frieze,

THE FIRST TCHATRALIS.

a sword at the end of his shoulder belt, like the soldiers of the first French Republic, a flintlock gun, a knife stuck into his waistband, and his feet bound up with strips of leather.

The boy is twelve or thirteen, with fair hair and blue eyes; his hair, which is cut short in front, falling over his shoulders. His only clothing is a cloak of white wool, and he is barefooted. He acts as interpreter for the man, translating what he says into indifferent Persian.

He asks me whence I came, who I am, and if I am not Ourousse (Russian), as he has been told by the Wakhis whom the Afghans have sent to him. I say that we are not Russians, but Feringhis.

"If you are, then you may proceed on your journey, for the Feringhis are *kheill doust* (very friendly) to Aman el Mulk, our *metar* (prince). But we are not friendly with the Russians, Chinese, or Afghans, and we have orders not to let them pass, even if we have to use force."

"We are neither Russians, Afghans, or Chinese, but Feringhis."

"Feringhi-Inglis?"

"No; Feringhis pure and simple, but very friendly to the English, in proof of which you see that we are making for Hindustan. Our great wish is to reach Guilguit and to see the English. We have lost our horses and their burdens in the snow. The Chinese are not our friends, for they wanted to kill us, nor are the Afghans, for they tried to stop us, and we fled from them without being able to get anything we required. As a general rule, people do not venture into a hostile country unless they are more numerous than we are. Besides myself, there are two Feringhis and two followers, or five in all. We must have felt convinced that we should be well received and be animated by the best intentions to come and see you with so small an escort."

This man seems struck by what I say, and after discussing for a few moments with the boy, who also appears to favour us, he determines to go on in advance and announce our arrival to his master, who is at a few days' march. He calls out to some men who are higher up the mountain, and they come down to show us the way.

Our little band has collected, and we go on all together to Top-Khana, the first hamlet upon the right bank of the Arkhun, arriving there in the evening, having met on the way a Karaul chief, who puts the same questions to us and to whom we make the same replies.

Upon May 17th, we leave Top-Khana, inhabited by Wakhis, who fled from their country when it was seized by the Afghans.

The inhabitants let us six donkeys to carry our baggage, which is reduced to a very small quantity. We start in good spirits, after having regaled ourselves on an omelette, some very diminutive chickens, and sour milk. We see some sheep which weigh about ten pounds, with cattle in proportion, the cows being about the size of an average calf, and the donkeys small but sturdy. The few horses in the country are imported from the Badakshan.

We go along the left bank of the river and reach a delightful wood, in the glades of which is plenty of grass. We stop to let our horses feed, and, stretched out upon the grass, we say to ourselves that our troubles are over and that in another month we shall be at Kashmir. Our troubles and difficulties are over, if the Tchatralis do not give us annoyance.

Suddenly a horse comes close up to us showing signs of fear, so that there must be a man or a wild animal close, for our horses are so wild that they prick their ears at the least sound, and are as good as watch-dogs to us. In a few moments, a number of men come in sight, and with their cross-belts, their plaited hair and smooth faces, they look like so many brown owls, or would do so but for their shields studded with bright nails and their profusion of arms. As it is, they remind one rather of characters in a comic opera, or Tziganes dressed as brigands and showing their white teeth. Their chief, who is on horseback, carries a rifle and a revolver. He says that he is the son of a very important personage, and that he has orders not to let us pass. We ask him if he has any one in his party who can speak Persian, and when he replies in the negative, we say that this is a great pity, as we have some very interesting papers to show him, but that we will go on and see his father, whom we shall have no difficulty in persuading that we are honest men. We give him a host of reasons in support of our allegation, and after consulting with his followers, he consents. We have not a boot to our feet, but though our dress was not calculated to inspire any one with a great idea of us, our arms and our defiant attitude may have caused respect. Certainly, we were not very taking in appearance, with our chapped hands and faces, the skin peeling off in places and making us look like lepers.

The worst of it was that we had no rupees, and only a little gold; and the young man argued, not without some show of reason, that if we were Feringhis we should be able to give him rupees. This is the ethnological sign by which the Tchatralis recognize the Feringhis-Inglis, as we found out afterwards. We encamped that evening at Dibarga, in a glade, the Tchatralis bivouacking quite close. The Wakhis of Top-Khana advised us to be on our guard, as the Tchatralis were deceitful and dishonest.

The next day (May 18), still following the left bank, now in the bed of the river, now upon the bank, we reached a hippodrome just outside Derbend, where we found the father of the young man, seated amid a circle of warriors.

TCHATRALI.

He had a parasol over his head, and his large moustaches came right across his face, from the chin of which hung a pointed beard. With much dignity, he asked us the same questions which his son had put to us the day before, and we answered them in the same way. He gave us to understand that he expected presents of rupees, and we gave *him* to understand that we were only in the habit of giving presents to our friends, and that we did not yet know with whom we had to do.

We then went to the foot of the fortress, where we shared, myself and my four companions, a frugal meal served in the hollow of a shield, consisting of excellent bread and apricots, the kernels serving as a separate dish. While we were enjoying this, we were being plied with the most outlandish questions, to which we replied without contradicting ourselves at all. The curious part of the business was that the chief's interpreter spoke Turkish very well, having learnt it at Samarcand, where he had been for fifteen years as a slave, having been sold when quite a boy to a pilgrim, who had taken him to Kashgar and resold him to a man from Khokand, who had in turn sold him to an inhabitant of Samarcand. This man had regained his liberty when the Russians came into the country. He knew several acquaintances of Rachmed, but that did not help us, as the interpreter who had acted as intermediary for us when we made purchases had shown his regard for us by stealing several pieces of cloth.

In the evening, we encamp at Paour, upon the right bank, and we are in an enclosure upon the bank of a winding stream which flows over small sharp pebbles. The tiny squares of cultivated land are bordered by trim paths, at the edges of which are willows and small walls made of stones. There are small cuttings made at various points for the purposes of irrigation, and everything is kept as neat and tidy as a Dutch farm. The inhabitants, however, only do just enough work to keep themselves going, for they are of a lazy disposition.

Their principal occupations are to comb their long hair, dye the corners of their eyes, pull the hairs out of their nostrils, and look at themselves in small mirrors. They seem to be very gentle and polite in their manners to one another, and there does not appear to be any distinct demarcation of rank—not, at all events, among the men who escort us.

They are fairly civil to us, as soon as they have unbosomed themselves of their threats, which they appear to have learnt by heart. One of them having said something rude to Menas, I advise the latter to give him a good hiding, which he does with a will, much to the astonishment of the others, who after this treat us with no little respect.

Despite the messengers sent by the Metar of Tchatral and his son, we have pursued our journey. Every now and again, a horseman came up and enjoined us to proceed no further, and our body of carriers stopped at least twenty times and put down our baggage, in compliance with superior instructions. But each time

MASTUDJ.

I got them to go on by recourse to the same arguments. Our superiority over these barbarians was due to the fact that we knew what we wanted, and they were vacillating.

Once at Mastudj, we pitched our tent in the sort of hippodrome or racecourse which extends along the cultivated ground on the river's bank and at the foot of several stone walls. This was a very large meadow, at the entrance to which stands out prominently the fortress inhabited by the second son of the prince who rules the country. This fortress, built of stones without mortar, separated by timber beams, is protected upon the side of the river by a ravine, at the foot of which are some marsh meadows, with pools of water all over them.

We halted here on May 22nd, and Rachmed, who is very fond of counting the days, reminds us that it is the 78th since we left Osch and the 143rd since we started from Samarcand, which he wonders whether he will ever see again. Rachmed wishes himself anywhere but where he is, for his stomach is quite upset, and he has a longing to eat kouirouk, that is, the fat of sheeps' tails.

Our little band is worn out, and the six horses left are so many bags of bones. We have scarcely any money left to pay for the conveyance of what little baggage we possess as far as Kashmir. We have to pay exorbitant prices, bread costing us nearly one shilling per pound, while our carriers insist upon eight shillings a day, and then five of them do not carry more than what one could fairly take on his back.

According to the information given us by the natives, we learn that there is an agent of the Anglo-Indian Government accredited to the Metar of Tchatral, and it is to him that we propose to apply and ask him to send a line from us to the Viceroy of India, who, we are sure, will help us out of the difficulty.

We rest for four days, collecting, during that period, a few provisions from the subject portion of the population. The Metar of Tchatral, who has committed almost every crime, has taken the place of the ruler of Mastudj, after having put him to death. There remain some few friends of the former order of things, and they are well inclined to us, or at all events they do not obey so blindly the orders of the new ruler. So they bring us some flour secretly.

At the end of four days, we load our horses as if we were going to start, and some men sent by the young prince come and beg us to wait a little, as their master is about to come and try to arrange something with us. He soon comes, followed by an escort armed with flintlocks, English sporting guns, and a few rifles. He is dressed in a robe of white cotton, and rides a white horse, his servitors making a great fuss over him as he gets off. He is about twenty-two or twenty-three, short, very dark, and with a black beard. He resembles a native of Bokhara, with his wandering look, thick lips, and stuttering utterance. He has on his feet some heavy Peshawur boots.

After an exchange of compliments, he plies us with the same questions as to our identity and plans, and when we persist in wishing to start, he overwhelms us with assurances of his affection for us, but does not want us to leave until he has received orders from his father. He says that if he lets us go, it will cost him his head, and he entreats us to wait a week till he has been to consult with his father at Tchatral. When he has been there, he will be able to provide us with plenty of men and beasts of burden, and he will himself carry us on his back, if necessary. But a visit must first be paid to the Metar at Tchatral, for it is the custom of the country, and the English have never failed to observe it.

THE METAR.

After a sitting which lasted several hours and exhausted the patience of Rashmed and Menas, we give way, the young prince declaring that we had better cut his head off at once if we persist in starting. The only condition we make is that we shall be well fed in the interval, and to this he readily assents, thanking us very profusely for having saved him any unpleasantness.

We know too well the value of Oriental promises to expect much, but the situation is at all events clearer than ever before, for it is evident that the Tchatralis, deny it as they may, take their orders from India, nor can they be altogether blamed for their denial, as it is well understood that they only execute the orders which they judge to be to their advantage.

We have nothing to do but wait for a reply to the letter we

VIEW IN THE VALLEY OF TCHATRAL.

have sent to the English agent. I do not tell him all the reasons we have for wishing to go forward, the first and most urgent being that the snow is melting, that the Mastudj river is no longer fordable, nor is the Wakhan-Darya. We have no longer the necessary strength to enter upon a fresh struggle against man and against nature, nor the money to buy the Tchatral—which is for sale.

My conviction is that nothing will be settled for weeks, as the letter we have sent will pass through several hands, and who can tell if it will ever reach its destination, for the Peshawur road is not very safe.

The Anglo-Indian Government can have no interest that we know of to bar the way for us, or to get the Tchatralis to cut our throats. And even if, for some stupid political reason, there is a reluctance to hold out a helping hand, we need not give up hope, for we would make some desperate attempt; and if we perished in it, well, we should have seen a good deal of the world.

So far luck has been with us, and now we must look back upon the various difficulties we have surmounted, and await with confidence the decision of the Anglo-Indian Government.

MAFUCH KAFIR.

On May 26th, Capus, Pepin, and Menas, start for Tchatral, Rachmed and myself remaining behind with our baggage and our worn-out horses. The young prince having opined that our baggage must not be conveyed there, it was easy to see that we should go in the direction, not of Peshawur, but of Laspour, whenever we were allowed to leave at all. We could not leave our baggage and horses with the natives, nor could we leave Rachmed alone, for if he took to smoking haschisch, or if he fell ill, what would become of him? Pepin cannot remain here, because he does not speak Russian, nor can Capus, as he dislikes being alone, and is anxious to see Tchatral. So it is settled that I shall stay behind.

The worthy Rachmed and myself, with our two dogs, remained at Mastudj forty-five days, and I did not find the time long, for, apart from the various incidents which broke the monotony of existence, there is no little interest in studying the manners and customs of a savage horde in such an out-of-the-way part of the world.

Upon May 28th, I receive a letter from the English agent at Tchatral, saying that he cannot let me start without an order from the English Government. This agent is a scribe of Afghan origin, who writes English more or less imperfectly. So there is nothing for it but to wait patiently.

TCHATRALI WOMAN AND WARRIOR.

These people do not live, but vegetate, the women doing all the work. They are lean and bony, with regular features, very dark-skinned, and they wear drawers and long loose coats of frieze. It is only the rich of both sexes who wear under garments of cotton, made after the Turkestan fashion, a loose garment with two wide sleeves and an opening in front.

They are fond of flowers, and wear them in their hair, and pay great attention to their heads, this being about the only part of their body which they do wash. Not but what there is plenty of good water, only they are content to drink it and watch it flow.

There is little or nothing in their empty heads, and once they have satisfied their modest animal tastes, they are quite content. They are as happy as possible when once they have appeased their hunger, and I often wonder whether our Western mania for "civilizing" other races, is calculated to improve the lot of the savages, as we call them.

The natives belong to a special sect, being neither Shiites nor Sunnis. They are, however, something like the latter, as they detest the Shiites of Guilguit and Yassin, who carry about the image of the Caliph Omar on a donkey. These people are "maoulani," that is to say, they shave their faces and foreheads, wear long hair and pray in a particular way.

The young prince goes occasionally to play polo, and his appearance is accompanied with considerable pomp. He comes from the fortress, which is about a mile and a quarter from my tent, surrounded by armed men, with a drummer preceding the party. When he plays with his horsemen and makes a good stroke, the gallery applauds to the echo. The polo ground is in the corner of the valley, about three hundred yards from my tent, and it is over a quarter of a mile long.

TCHATRALI.

He has paid me three visits, which I have not returned. In the short conversations which we have had in Persian, upon the felt stretched in front of the tent, I have been able to see how ignorant he is. He cannot even read correctly, or write, and he knows nothing about any books except the Koran, which is occasionally read to him, and the Shah-Nameh of Firdousi. He has not read it, but he has been told that there is such a book, and that it is a very interesting one.

He knows the names of neighbouring princes, such as Nadir-Shah, and though he does not know Baber, he puts his hand up to his mouth as if to reflect, and says that Baber must be the man who brought his family into the Tchatral, and must be of his line. He knows that Tchinguiz-Khan was a Mogul, and as to Iskander (Alexander), he supposes him to have been a good Mussulman.

This young man with five wives is not rich, so he is not able to keep his family in much affluence: bread, rice, and mutton once a week, such is the food of the garrison, as it appears.

So we have some difficulty in obtaining what is strictly necessary for ourselves. We have to complain every day, and ask for more wood, more flour, and more meat. We cannot get any salt, and the head cook, to whom Rachmed complains, thinks that we eat a great deal too much. We have refused an old goat, whose teeth are loose in his head, and we insist upon sheep. After long discussion, they agree to give us one every other day. This will enable us to have meat once a day, a sheep weighing from five to seven pounds.

TCHATRALI.

Rachmed says that these sheep are not so good as the goats in his own country, and that an Uzbeg would not eat them.

We obtain what we require by resorting to two threats, one to the young prince, whom I tell that we are going to start for Guilguit, and that before doing so we shall make a good meal upon the first cow we come across, for if we are to be treated as malefactors, the best way is to go the whole hog. Then, whenever any promise is made us, we bring our influence to bear upon the slave who comes with the provisions each evening at sunset, and who is very afraid of our two dogs, which we have trained to go for the legs of any visitors who have not announced their coming. We tell him that if he does not bring the promised sheep in the morning, we will have him eaten up by the two dogs, and the slave, who is not a marvel of intelligence, quite believes it.

As we treated this poor fellow very kindly, in reality, he became our fast friend.

The days passed very monotonously, and in the morning we let out the horses, except two stallions, whom the vicinity of a number of mares rendered very intractable and prevented from feeding. In the evening, the horses returned of their own accord, and we gave them a little chopped straw, which was all we had to give them. We then hobbled them, and saw to the wounds on their backs.

TCHATRALI.

When the natives did not bring us any straw, we tethered them in the grass, and the next morning the owners of the pastures complained, coming to us and getting their calves bitten by our dogs. We then told them that they must go and complain to their master, whose fault it was that our horses had no provender, and in this way we obtained the respect of these men, who were convinced that we must be important personages.

A month of fasting among the natives was followed by festivals, in the course of which the children ate coloured eggs, and one of the exiles enabled us to take part in these rejoicings by sending us a pound or two of a sort of pasty made of butter and sour milk.

TCHATRALI SOLDIER.

On the ground where polo is played, the people assembled to witness several wrestling matches. The prince was present, and distributed the prizes to the winners, these prizes consisting of pieces of cotton stuff from Manchester or the Punjab.

One of the wrestlers, who had shown great power, was detected two days later in a flagrant act of adultery and was stabbed to death by the angry husband. The wife escaped with a beating, her lord and master's reason for showing mercy being that she did all the work of the house. When angry, a man may kill his neighbour's dog that has stolen a piece of his meat; but if it is his own dog, he is content with giving him a good kick.

This occurrence created no little sensation, and we saw people climbing up to the roofs of the houses and looking down upon the place where the tragedy had taken place, while in the open air were groups collected to exchange their ideas on the subject.

TCHATRALI DANCER.

The cemetery of Mastudj is situated upon the right bank, upon a platform overlooking the stream, and at the foot of the steep mountain. It is surrounded by a wall, the top of which is surmounted by sharp spikes, and it was there that the dead man was interred, stark naked, and with his face turned towards the Kebla. The dead at Mastudj are always stripped of their garments, because this country is so poor that a pair of cotton drawers or a frieze coat are often about all the dead man has left. I saw that the friends of the defunct fetched some stones from the nearest spot and placed them upon his tomb.

The man who had slain him went to tell the prince what had occurred, and came back to eat a dish of mulberries under the shade of his father-in-law's apricot tree. And so the matter ended, according to the custom of the country.*

We obtain some information as to what is going on in the fortress, thanks to a Swat vendor, who has come to sell cotton goods in this part of the Tchatral. He comes every year at the same period, with goods from Manchester and the Punjab, and as money is almost an unknown commodity in this country he exchanges his goods for woollen cloaks very well woven, and donkeys upon which he loads them, selling both the cloaks and the donkeys in the north of the Punjab and the Swat. He is a tall and thin old man, with a long beard, quite of the Afghan type and speaking Persian fluently. He is very happy in Rachmed's society, and the latter is very fond of a good gossip. Being himself a foreigner, he makes friends all the more readily with us, who are strangers as well, especially as we receive him very kindly and give him a present of some value; while he is very dissatisfied with the young prince who has purchased a large part of his goods and keeps putting him off for the payment of them.

TCHATRALI.

The trader, finding time hang heavy on his hands in the fortress, went out from time to time under the pretext of feeding his two donkeys, and made his way by a roundabout route to our tent. As soon as we saw him coming, we chained up the dogs, so that they might not bark and warn the natives that he was coming to see us.

* NOTE OF THE TRANSLATOR.—Very much the same ending as such affairs have in France, where a form of trial is gone through, I am well aware; but it ends in an acquittal, as a matter of course.

One day, just as Rachmed made the thirty-fifth notch on the tent pole, the old man came to tell us that messengers on foot had arrived from Kashmir, with letters for the Metar of Tchatral. These letters contained orders that we were to be treated kindly and our journey into India facilitated. This was good news, and the truth of it was confirmed the same evening, when a servitor of the young prince brought us two pounds of excellent butter, wrapped up in the bark of a birch-tree, from the fat pasturages of the upper valley of Arkhun.

TCHATRALI MOLLAH.   MIGANE AT TCHATRAL.

This pat of butter seemed to us a sign of the times, presaging, like a comet in the sky, events of great importance.

The next day I sent Rachmed to the fortress, to ask the young prince for a cup, under the pretext that we had broken our last and that we had to drink with our hands.

He was very politely received, not by the prince himself, who, as he was told, was having his reading lesson from the mollah who was completing his much-neglected education, but by the courtiers. After waiting an hour to no purpose, he came back and said—

" I have been all this time squatted upon the reeds (which are the carpet of the country). I was among the chief personages of the court, who plied me with questions. They were all picking out fleas from under their clothes, and as I had managed to get a cup, and do not like these insects, I came away."

KAFIR.

The cup which he had brought was made of Kashgar porcelain, but it was too small, so Rachmed mended ours a second time, using paper and apricot sap for cement.

On the same day, a man from Asmar, who had been sent by his khan on a mission to the young prince of Mastudj, came to wish us good-bye and ask for a remedy for toothache. The Swat trader, who had acted as interpreter to him, and who had been blind in one eye for fifteen years, took advantage of the same opportunity to ask us if we had not some ointment which would restore his sight. We explained to him that there were certain ailments which could only be cured by Allah, that man has to learn to bear his burden, and that when death comes to deliver him of it, it seems a light one.

The Asmari thought that I had spoken wisely, and when I had given him a letter for our companions at Tchatral—which he delivered safely—he went striding off, his hands gripping the ends of his sword, which he had placed at the back of his neck. This man, with his tall figure, oval head, hooked nose, and shaven forehead, was more like an Arab chief, and had all the dignity of one. He was dressed in a short white cotton shirt and a pair of drawers, each leg as loose as a skirt, these latter being very pleasant wear in summer, as I can testify. He wore Peshawur slippers, and professed the utmost contempt for the Tchatralis, calling them shameless beggars.

Rachmed was very tired of waiting, and at times I had great difficulty in preventing him from going off. When he was in this state of exasperation, so often found in people who are accustomed to great activity, and who are suddenly reduced to absolute inaction, he came to me and gave expression to his complaints. I listened patiently to the advice he gave me that I should kill a Tchatrali chief, steal his horses, and ride off at full speed, changing horses whenever an opportunity offered, hamstringing those which might be used to pursue us, and so forth. Then I turned the conversation into some other channel, and I invariably calmed him down by telling him some story from La Fontaine (whose fables interested him very much) or some other author.

Rachmed had just cut the forty-second notch in the pole of

our tent, and was lamenting our ill-luck, when he saw behind the hedge, about fifty yards off, the head of the trader, who was making signs to him to fasten up the dogs, which were asleep beside us. He then came up and told us that three men had arrived from Guilguit by forced marches, and that they brought

KAFIR.

with them letters from the Viceroy, which were to be delivered into our own hands, that we had been expected for the last fortnight at Guilguit, and that these messengers were going to Tchatral to fetch our companions as soon as they had rested themselves a little, for they had come in five days, and their feet were all to pieces.

The dove bearing this olive-branch soon appeared, in the form of a little Afghan, dressed in a white cotton robe, very sunburnt, and, as we thought, full of energy and intelligence. He hands us letters dated from Simla, and gives various information to Rachmed, who literally drinks in his words. He tells us that he is at our service, and that if we wish it, he will start off at once for Tchatral, but that he is scarcely in a condition to walk far, as we may see by his feet. We tell him to take a little breathing-space, kill a sheep in his honour, and do the best we can for him. He tells us that the road is very bad, very stony, and very trying, but that he shall travel it with pleasure upon the return to Kashmir, for this country is a nest of thieves, and if he had to spend a week at Mastudj he should fall ill.

MAN OF YAGUISTAN.

This is quite true, for the place we have inhabited for the last six weeks has, owing to the heavy rains, become a pestilential marsh. It is a regular hot-bed of fever, and it is a miracle that I have not been attacked at all, and Rachmed only slightly, while the teeth of the natives are chattering and their bodies shivering all around us.

The Viceroy sends us a very polite letter, written by his secretary, Sir D. Mackenzie Wallace, and Mr. Durand sends us another, written in English, in which he says that general orders have been issued to facilitate our journey and save us all discomfort. Nothing could possibly be better.

Two days later, the little Afghan starts for Tchatral, and I then have an altercation with the prince's prime minister, who persists in refusing us horses and guides upon the pretext that he cannot act without orders from his father. We are tired of this aping of discipline and omnipotence, and we formally call upon him, on behalf of the Viceroy, whose seal is familiar to him, to have a caravan ready by the 9th of July, that is to say, the forty-ninth day after our arrival at Mastudj. After much fencing, he eventually gives way, when I have explained to him by a regular Oriental comparison that "the Tchatral is to India what a *magiac* (fly) is under a horse's belly. As long as the fly does not sting much, the horse pays no heed to it. But if it gets troublesome, the horse crushes it with a stamp of the foot."

KASHMIR SCRIBE.

So, on the 9th of July, having been seized with an attack of sciatica the day before, I make Rachmed draw on some boots made of a horse's skin, which he had manufactured for me the previous day. He sets me upright, helps me on to a horse, and off we start. Two days later, my back was quite well again, so true is it that motion is the best of doctors, at all events for travellers, and we had plenty of it up to the end of September.

We reached the other side of the Laspour pass without any great difficulty in procuring donkeys and carriers. Once in the ill-defined region which is called the Punial, and on which the Khan of Yassin is said to exercise a certain amount of influence, we met some Kashmir soldiers escorting a bag of rupees, sent us by the Anglo-Indian Government. After getting beyond the hamlet of Teru, we had to skirmish with some very barbarian and talkative people, of whom our Kashmir escort stood in great fear. They said that we were in the Yaguistan, and they

FORTRESS OF GARKUCH.

pronounced the word with fear and trembling, as much as to tell us we must be on our guard. The name of Yaguistan is given to the whole country inhabited by independent tribes. I need not describe in detail the incidents of the journey. At one time, the carriers would throw their loads on the ground; at another, the villagers, with whom we had held a long discussion as to the price we were to pay them for their services, eventually promising them two or three times what they were

BUNGALOW OF MAJOR BIDDULPH AT GILGIT.

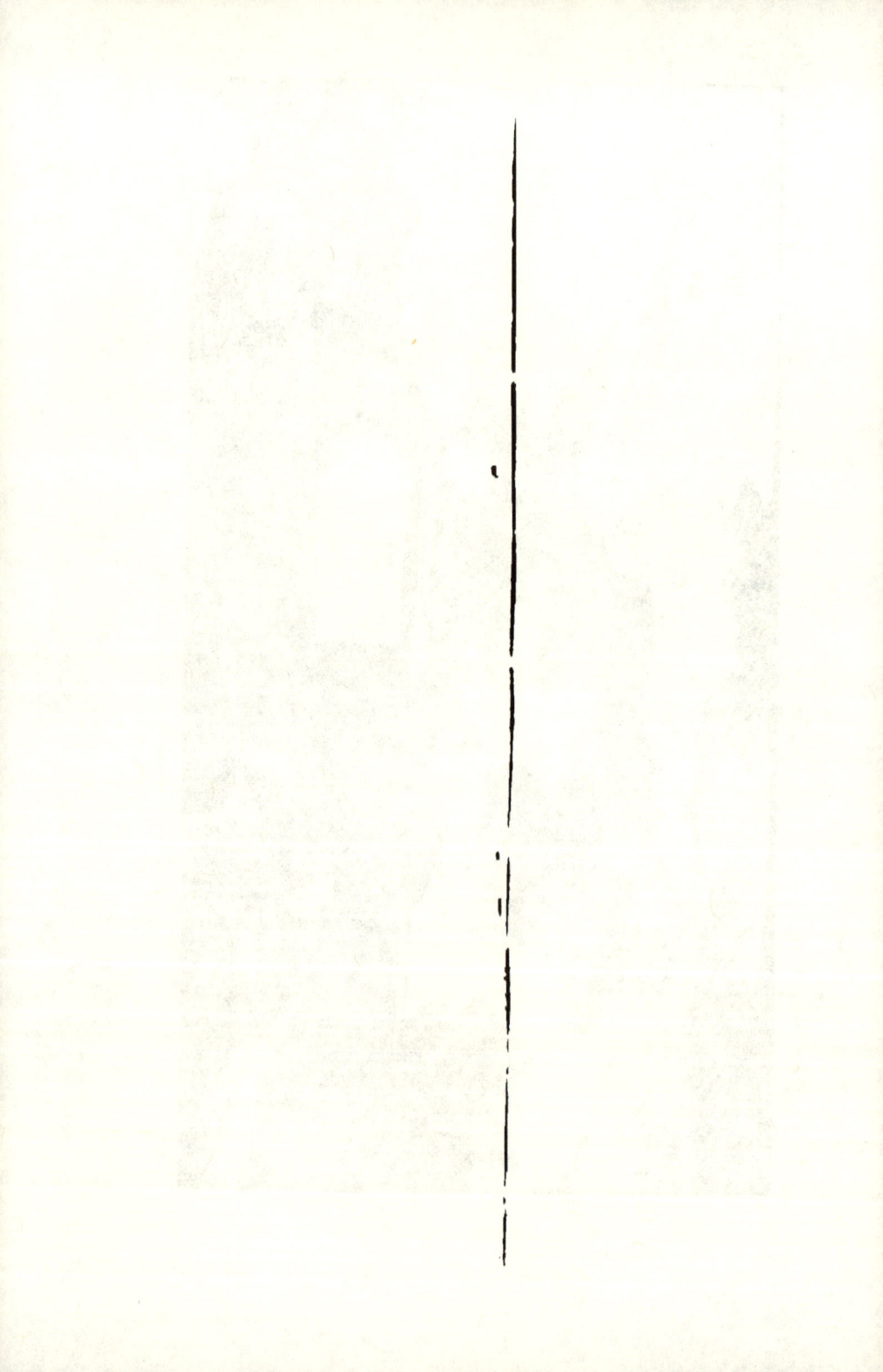

worth, refused the next morning to have anything to do with us. They assembled around us, fully armed, gesticulating and uttering threats. I picked out in the crowd the chiefs, whose beards were dyed with henna, the most venerable of the whole group, and in a trice I got them together, with the help of Rachmed. With a revolver ready to fire, and by the application of a few blows with a stick, we got them to order their men to obey us, under fear of having their noses taken off. The men of Kashmir, emboldened by our example, helped to keep the others in order, and the elders, seeing that we were in earnest, adopted the wisest course, and made their men reload the baggage and go on to the next stage, where the same scene was re-enacted.

The winter route, which is the easier of the two, had disappeared, for the ice over which one passes in cold weather had melted when the warm weather first set in, and before the rivers have risen, travellers go along their beds, but now that the rainy season had set in, we were obliged to scramble along goatpaths.

It is in this way that we arrived, by Gupis, in Kashmir territory, awaiting at Gahkuch our travelling companions. The junction was effected on the 20th of July, and, after our joyful meeting, we went by double stages to Guilguit, where we were lodged in the bungalow of Major Biddulph, by the order of the native governor.

After five days spent in repose and in letter writing, we left Guilguit on the 29th of July, having paid a visit to the modest tomb of Hayward, which is overshadowed by willows and vines, the overlapping foliage of which forms a very charming canopy for the "gallant officer and accomplished traveller," as the inscription upon it designates him. All around the tomb, there is a babble of water trickling upon a meadow as green as those in England, and it murmurs so gently that there is no fear of its awakening the plucky traveller who fell a victim to brigands. It is better that he should not be disturbed in his sleep, for thus he will not hear what the Geographical Society of London says about him, in fulfilment of the proverb that "the absent are always in the wrong."

On the 11th of August, we embarked upon Lake Srinagar, in a boat rowed by men who resembled the Sarthians of Turkestan, and by women who remind one of certain Italian types.

We remained at Kashmir just long enough to get a fresh

WOMAN OF KASHMIR.

outfit; we had abandoned our two last horses at three days' march from there, but we had all our men with us, very poor in condition, but in comparative good health, and glad at having succeeded.

M. Dauvergne, who had sent us some provisions which we had received a few stages before reaching Kashmir, offered us a generous hospitality, and, thanks to the kindness of other fellow-countrymen, such as MM. Peychaud, Fabre and Bouley, we could fancy ourselves back in France. The delusion was a pardonable one, for M. Peychaud gave us some excellent Burgundy, the produce of some Bordeaux vines which the climate had transformed. Having said good-bye to these kind friends, as soon as we had got our outfits, we started for Rawul-Pindi, and so by rail and coach to Simla, where we went to thank Lord Dufferin, whose family and staff received us most kindly. It was there that we learnt that M. de Balachoff, a generously disposed Russian residing in Paris, had interested himself in our fate, and had sent a sum of £240 for us to draw upon.

From Simla, we went to embark at Kurrachee on the 1st of September, escaping the cholera, so that we were fortunate to the end. At Port Saïd, we parted company with Menas and Rachmed, who went home by way of Constantinople and Batum.

By the end of September, we had got back to our homes, having completed this last part of our journey as I have said before, "with the rapidity of a bird returning to its nest."

INDIAN OF KURRACHEE.

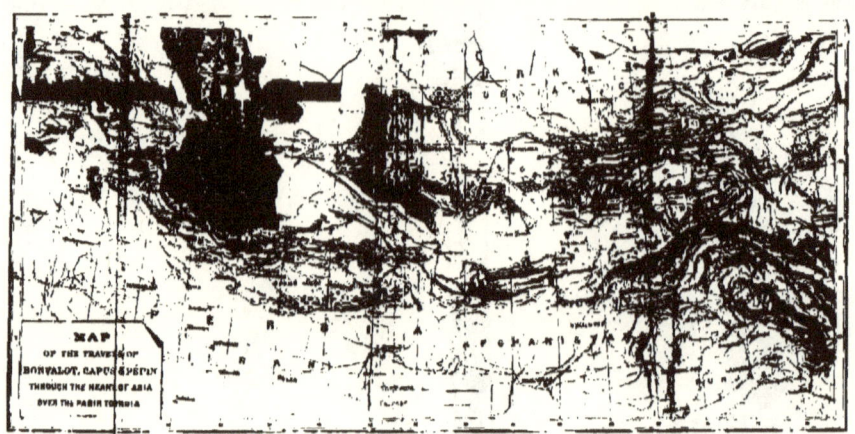

INDEX.

Abbas-Abad, i. 130
Abdul-Kerim, i. 219
Abdullah-Abad, i. 113
Abdurrhaman-Khan, i. 262
Afghans, among the, i. 240-273
Akbaltal, ii. 93
Ak-Basoga, ii. 43, 51, 54
Ak-Beles, the gorge of, ii. 182
Akmetchet, i. 238
Ak-Salir, ii. 119
Aksu, the river, ii. 27, 151, 174
Ak-Tach, ii. 129, 152-163
Alaï, the, i. 36
Alalan, the village of, i. 79
Alhak, i. 130
Alikhanoff, i. 185
Amman-Kutan, i. 198
Amu, crossing the river, i. 248
Anatolie, the, i. 1
Andreieff, i. 32
Annenkoff, General, i. 181
Antelopes, i. 166
Aouvan, i. 114
Aphrosiab, ruins of, ii. 7
Ardaban, i. 108
Arka, ii. 8
Arkhun, the, ii. 220
Aryk, the river, ii. 7
Askhabad, i. 181
Astara, i. 43
Atitchar, mountain, ii. 180

Baba, the, i. 107, 108
Bachkala, i. 238

Baïssounne, ii. 21
Bala-Guizine, ii. 193
Balkh, ii. 2
Balloy, De, French Minister at Teheran, i. 25, 98
Baroguil, the pass of, ii. 209
Basal-Gumbaz, ii. 52, 154, 181
Batir-Beg, ii. 49
Batoum, i. 18
Bazaar, a Turkish, i. 4
Beïkara, ii. 188
"Best" at Reshd, the, i. 91 ; at Meshed, i. 156
Bir-Kutdja, the, ii. 181
Birds, i. 42
Bishkent, i. 242
Bokhara, i. 186
Boschell, Captain, i. 2, 20
Bosphorus, the, i. 10
Bostan, i. 101, 125-127
Bread, i. 83
British Boundary Commission, the, i. 228, 257

Cabul, i. 222
Café de l'Hellespont, the, i. 3
Camels, i. 244 ; two-humped, ii. 10
Caravansary, a, i. 104, 145
Chahabad, i. 147
Chahr-Sabz, i. 198
Chak-Agatch, i. 43
Chaksevem Tartars, i. 67
Chattput, ii. 144
Chifa-Rud, i. 81

INDEX.

Churab, i. 140
Constantinople, i. 6
Cyanide of potassium, i. 280

Dachtighaz, ii. 21
Dahana, village, i. 207
Damgan, i. 118
Dancing man, a Persian, i. 102
Daouletabad, i. 116
Darcot, the glacier of, ii. 209
Dardanelles, the, i. 2
Dchangab-Darya, i. 221
De Balloy, French Minister at Teheran, i. 25, 98
Debimollah, i. 130
Dehinemek, village, i. 108, 111
Deibner, Colonel, ii. 54
Dennissoff, Lieutenant, i. 175
Derbend, ii. 25
Dibarda, ii. 225
Djame, ii. 29
Djangrik, ii. 59
Djar-Kurgane, ii. 7
"Djiguitovka," a, i. 28
Djizak, ii. 35
Djuma Mosque at Veramine, the, i. 97
Durand, Mr., ii. 242

Eivani-Keif, i. 102
Enzeli, town, i. 84
Exorcism, an, i. 277

Faker-Daout, i. 149
Felt boots, ii. 41
Fever, i. 65, 202

Gabkuch, ii. 247
Galberg, Captain, ii. 57
Gallípoli, i. 6
Gazelles, i. 166, 168
Ghuzalane, ii. 171
Gluchanovski, Captain, ii. 56, 67
Goat-skin game, the, ii. 8, 25
Golden Horn, the, i. 6
Grombtchefski, Captain, ii. 36, 48, 56
Guilan, the "land of mud," i. 32
Guk-Set, river, ii. 108

Gultcha, ii. 56, 57
Gupis, ii. 247
Guzar, ii. 26

Hadji Cabul, i. 27
Hazret-Sultan, mountain, ii. 27
Hecatompylos, site of, i. 126
Hissar, i. 213-227

Iamba (silver bars), ii. 46
Ichiki, valley, ii. 126
Imam Riza, the, i. 148
Iochkh, ii. 214
Irkestame, ii. 38
Irmenatag, ii. 171

Kabardiane, i. 238
Kabut-Gumbaz, station, i. 98
Kacha, i. 116
Kadamga, i. 148
Kafirnagane, river, i. 239, 243
Kaflan-Kul, ii. 56
Kakalti, ii. 7
Kaladagni, i. 43
Kalta-Kul, i. 206
Kalta Minor, ii. 26
Kamara-Tag, ii. 126
Kamaroff, General, i. 172, 181
Karabag, ii. 26
Karabuga, i. 159
Kara-Kul, Lake, ii. 54
Karakurum, the passes of, ii. 35
Karalkoff, General, i. 198; ii. 32, 36
Kara-Su, valley, ii. 144
Karatag, i. 212, 219
Kargalik, ii. 35
Karganrud, i. 48, 79
Karkaval, ii. 26
Karys, underground canals, i. 118
Karzan, i. 94
Kashgar, ii. 32, 35
Kashmir, ii. 248
Kastakos, ii. 35
Katti-Kurgane, i. 195
Katun-Rabad, i. 244
Kauffmann, General, i. 198
Kauffmann peak, the, ii. 82

INDEX. 253

Kchef, the river, i. 159
Ketchidar, village, i. 162
Khevir, i. 48; the steppe, i. 103
Khodjend, ii. 35
Khodjikara, river, i. 46
Khokand, ii. 35
Khorassan, province, i. 116
Kich-Kupruk, ii. 11
Kila-Pandj, ii. 219
Kishlak, i. 103, 104
Kizelkurgane, ii. 58
Kizil-Agatch, i. 35
Kizil-Aguin, the, ii. 82, 89, 100
Kizil-Art, pass, ii. 36-39; river, ii. 82, 100
Kizil-Djek, pass, ii. 119
Kizil-Djilgua, ii. 137
Kizil-Korum, ii. 172
Kizil-Kul, ii. 107
Kizil-Uzen, river, i. 92
Kudum, i. 92
Kum, i. 35
Kumbachi, i. 35
Kum-Kurghane, ii. 11
Kunjut, ii. 36, 129, 146, 153, 174
Kurds, i. 16, 94
Kurian, i. 119
Kus-Khan, ruins of, i. 175

Ladak, ii. 35
Lagopodes, ii. 115
Langar, ii. 198
Langar-Su, valley, ii. 183
Laspour, ii. 231, 243
Lazguird, village, i. 11
Lebrun, M., i. 182
Lenkoran, i. 35
Lullis, i. 210

Madi, ii. 56
Maiakanes, the, i. 32
Marguilane, ii. 35, 36, 41
Markan-Su, valley, ii. 104
Marmora, Sea of, i.
Marseilles, i. 1
Mastudj, ii. 227-236
Mazari-Cherif, i. 241
Maziaan, village, i. 131

Mazraa, i. 94
Medicine, i. 76
Meiamei, oasis, i. 130
Mendjil, i. 93
Mercury frozen, ii. 135
Merv, i. 177
Meshed, i. 101, 152
Miandecht, i. 130
Minstrel, a Persian, i. 71
Mintout, ii. 10
Mirza-Murad, valley, ii. 183
Miskar, village, ii. 188
Mosque, an old, i. 98
Moustagata peak, the, ii. 125
Mus-Kalé, ii. 173
Mus-Kul, lake, ii. 119
Muiderane, i. 164

Naphtha (petroleum), i. 19
Namrabad, i. 142
Nichapur, i. 142
Nowrouz, festival of the, i. 31

Osch, ii. 41, 48
Oxus, the, ii. 151, 174

Pamir, the, ii. 32
Paouf, ii. 226
Patta-Kissar, ii. 3
Peri-Bazar, i. 85
Perikledasta, a, i. 28
Persia, the Shah of, i. 69
Petroleum, i. 19
Photography, i. 70, 82
Porters, Turkish, i. 9, 15
Poti, town, i. 19
Prichip, village, i. 32
Punial, the, ii. 244

Rabat-Sarpuch, i. 132
Rabut, ii. 181
Rages, i. 97-101
Railway, the, i. 228
Rakim-Khan, i. 48
Raleigh, Mr., of the *Standard*, i. 143
Rang-Kul, ii. 93, 110, 127
Refuge at Renhd, i. 91

INDEX.

Rei, i. 101
Repetek, i. 186
Reshd, i. 87
Rigar, i. 211, 225
Rion, town, i. 23
Road-making, Persian, i. 92
Rudbar, i. 93
Rukhabad, i. 173
Russian sectaries, i. 32
Rustamabad, i. 92

Sabzevar, i. 132
Saderabad, i. 131
Sadik, i. 113
Safid-Rud, river, i. 93
Saliane, town, i. 28
Salt mine, i. 238
Saltpetre-makers, i. 114
Salm, Colonel, i. 170
Samarcand, i. 186, 195; ii. 29, 31
Samson shepherd, a, i. 13
Sang-Kuk, ii. 214
Sanguirdak, valley, i. 206; village, i. 207
Sarakhs, i. 170
Sarhad, ii. 213
Saridjui, i. 207
Saxaoul (a shrub), i. 131
Shah, the, i. 69
Shahroud, i. 101, 125
Sherifabad, i. 102, 150
Shirabad mountains, the, ii. 9
Siah-Ab, source of the, ii. 189
Simnam, i. 114
Soldiers, Turkish, i. 4, 5
Sorcery, ii. 19
Srinagar, Lake, ii. 248
Stamboul, i. 9
Steppes, the, i. 25
Stevens, Mr., i. 142
Sturgeon fishery, i. 28
Sufi-Kurgane, ii. 59
Surkhane, the, i. 207; ii. 7
Sutkar, i. 131

Tachka-Karatcha, pass, i. 198
Tachtugal, ii. 11
Tagharma peak, the, ii. 125, 153

Taldik, the, ii. 37, 39
Talich, i. 54-57
Tartar laziness, i. 44
Tashkhurgan, i. 206; ii. 143
Tash-Kupruk, ii. 174, 188
Taskhend, ii. 41
Tchal, river, i. 103
Tchakma-Kultin, lake, ii. 176
Tchaktchak, pass, ii. 26
Tchardjui, i. 186
Tcharpatchal, i. 84
Tchatral, ii. 227-231
Tchef, river, i. 163
Tchilab, ii. 174, 181
Tchiraktchi, ii. 26
Tchochka-Guzar, i. 246; ii. 1
Tchotkal, the, i. 163
Tchulakbas, ii. 60
Tedjene, the, i. 167
Teheran, i. 97
Tekkes, the, i. 189, 190
Tengez-Bei, pass, ii. 37, 39
Terek-Davan, the, ii. 35-38
Termiz, ii. 2, 4
Tiflis, town, i. 20, 24
Tsiakent, village, i. 31
Top-Khana, ii. 223
Toura of Kissar, the, i. 205
Touradjane of Hissar, the, i. 230
Tous, i. 101
Trebizond, i. 15
Trout in the Tufalanque, i. 208
Tufalanque, river, i. 208
Turkomans, the, i. 115, 167, 193
Turks, the, i. 9, 15
Tuskane, valley, i. 238
Tuslak, i. 244
Tuyun-Murun, pass, ii. 38

Ura-Tepe, ii. 35
Urtak, ii. 90
Ustik Dalasu, ii. 153
Utch-Hadji, the well of, i. 189
Uzun-Djilga, ii. 121

Veramine, i. 97
Visna, i. 47

Wakhan, the, ii. 53, 129
Wallace, Mr. Mackenzie, ii. 242
Waterfowl, i. 35; ii. 166
Winter, preparing for, i. 210

Yaguistan, the, ii. 244
Yakabag, village, i. 198
Yakoob-Khan, i. 261

Yangiarik, i. 240
Yassin, ii. 203

Zaamin, ii. 35
Zarsotte, ii. 195
Zerabchane, river, i. 196
Zerafchane, river, ii. 35
Zumanabad, i. 140

A SELECTION FROM THE CATALOGUE

OF

CHAPMAN AND HALL'S PUBLICATIONS.

November 20, 1888.

SPORT AND TRAVEL.

THROUGH THE HEART OF ASIA OVER THE PAMIR TO INDIA.
By GABRIEL BONVALOT. With 250 Illustrations by ALBERT PÉPIN. 2 vols. Royal 8vo.
[*In December.*

LIFE ABOARD A BRITISH PRIVATEER IN THE TIME OF
QUEEN ANNE. Being the Journals of Captain Woodes Rogers, Master Mariner. With Notes and Illustrations by ROBERT C. LESLIE, Author of "A Sea-Painter's Log." Large crown 8vo. [*In December.*

ROUND ABOUT NEW ZEALAND. Being Notes from a Journal of Three Years' Wandering in the Antipodes. By E. W. PAYTON. With Twenty Original Illustrations by the Author. Large crown 8vo. 12s. [*In December.*

FROM CALAIS TO PEKIN BY LAND. By H. DE WINDT. With Numerous Illustrations by the Author. 2 vols. Demy 8vo. [*In December.*

POWDER, SPEAR, AND SPUR. By J. MORAY BROWN. With Illustrations. Crown 8vo. [*In December.*

ENGLISH AND AMERICAN YACHTS. Illustrating and Describing the most famous Yachts now sailing in English and American Waters. With a Treatise upon Yachts and Yachting. By EDWARD BURGESS. Illustrated with 50 Beautiful Photogravure Engravings. Oblong folio. 42s.

UNTRODDEN PATHS IN ROUMANIA. By Mrs. WALKER, Author of "Sketches of Eastern Life and Scenery," etc. With 77 Illustrations. Demy 8vo. 10s. 6d.

NORWEGIAN SKETCHES: FISHING IN STRANGE WATERS.
By EDWARD KENNARD. Illustrated with 30 beautiful Sketches printed by The Automatic Engraving Co. Oblong folio. 21s.
A SET OF SIX HAND-COLOURED PLATES, 21s. ; IN OAK FRAMES, 42s.

TIGER SHOOTING IN THE DOON AND ULWAR, AND LIFE IN
INDIA. By Lieut.-Col. J. C. FIFE-COOKSON. With numerous Illustrations by E. HOBDAY, R.H.A., from Sketches by the Author. Large crown 8vo. 10s. 6d.

SPORT: FOX HUNTING, SALMON FISHING, COVERT SHOOT-
ING, DEER STALKING. By the late W. BROMLEY-DAVENPORT, M.P. With numerous Illustrations by General CREALOCK, C.B. Crown 8vo. 3s. 6d.

TWENTY-FIVE YEARS IN A WAGGON IN THE GOLD REGIONS OF AFRICA. By ANDREW A. ANDERSON. With Illustrations and Map. Demy 8vo. 12s.

WITH THE CAMEL CORPS UP THE NILE. By Count GLEICHEN, Grenadier Guards. With numerous Sketches by the Author. Second Edition. Large crown 8vo. 9s.

HIGHWAYS AND HORSES. By ATHOL MAUDSLAY. With Numerous Illustrations. Demy 8vo. 21s.

SADDLE AND MOCASSIN. By FRANCIS FRANCIS, Jun. Crown 8vo. 12s.

SPORTS AND ANECDOTES OF BYGONE DAYS. In England, Scotland, Ireland, Italy, and the Sunny South. By C. T. S. BIRCH REYNARDSON. With Illustrations in colour. Second Edition. Large crown 8vo. 12s.

DOWN THE ROAD: REMINISCENCES OF A GENTLEMAN COACHMAN. By C. T. S. BIRCH REYNARDSON. With Coloured Illustrations. Demy 8vo. 12s.

COURT LIFE IN EGYPT. By A. J. BUTLER, Author of "The Ancient Coptic Churches of Egypt." With Illustrations. Demy 8vo. 12s.

SKETCHES OF LIFE IN JAPAN. By Major HENRY KNOLLYS, R.A. With Illustrations. Demy 8vo. 12s.

TRAVELS, SPORTS, AND POLITICS IN THE EAST. By the Marquis of HUNTLY. With Illustrations by the Marchioness of HUNTLY. Demy 8vo. 12s.

LOG-BOOK OF A FISHERMAN AND ZOOLOGIST. By FRANK BUCKLAND. With numerous Illustrations. Fifth Thousand. Crown 8vo. 5s.

THE ANCIENT CITIES OF THE NEW WORLD. Being Travels and Explorations in Mexico and Central America, 1857–1882. By DÉSIRÉ CHARNAY. Translated from the French by J. GONINO and HELEN S. CONANT. With upwards of 200 Illustrations. Super royal 8vo. 31s. 6d.

THE RACEHORSE IN TRAINING, with Hints on Racing and Racing Reform, to which is added a Chapter on Shoeing. By WILLIAM DAY. Fifth Edition. Demy 8vo. 9s.

A SEA-PAINTER'S LOG. By ROBERT C. LESLIE. With 12 full-page Illustrations by the Author. Large crown 8vo. 12s.

BIOGRAPHICAL.

MADAME DE STAËL. By Lady BLANNERHASSET. 3 vols. Demy 8vo.
[*In December.*

MEMOIRS OF A ROYALIST. By Count DE FALLOUX. Translated from the French by C. B. PITMAN. 2 vols. Demy 8vo. 32s.

THE LIFE OF THE RIGHT HON. W. E. FORSTER. By T. WEMYSS REID. 2 vols. Demy 8vo. Fourth Edition, with Portraits. 32s.

MODERN METHUSELAHS; or, Short Biographical Sketches of a few advanced Nonagenarians or actual Centenarians who were distinguished in Art, Science, Literature, or Philanthropy. Also brief notices of some individuals remarkable chiefly for their longevity. With an Introductory Chapter on "Long-lasting." By JOHN BURN BAILEY. Demy 8vo. 10s. 6d.

PRINCE EUGENE OF SAVOY. By Colonel G. B. MALLESON, C.S.I. With Portrait and Maps. Crown 8vo. 6s.

MUSIC AND MANNERS. Personal Reminiscences and Sketches of Character. By W. BEATTY-KINGSTON. Second Edition. 2 vols. Demy 8vo. 30s.

MONARCHS I HAVE MET. By W. BEATTY-KINGSTON. 2 vols. Demy 8vo. 24s.

A WANDERER'S NOTES. By W. BEATTY-KINGSTON. 2 vols. Demy 8vo. 24s.

MONTROSE. By Lady VIOLET GREVILLE. With an Introduction by the EARL OF ASHBURNHAM, containing Two Portraits. Large crown 8vo. 7s. 6d.

GEORGE WASHINGTON. By Major COOPER KING. Crown 8vo.
[In January.

VAUBAN, MONTALEMBERT, CARNOT: Engineer Studies. By E. M. LLOYD, Major R.E., late Professor of Fortification at the Royal Military Academy, Woolwich. With Portraits. Crown 8vo.

MEMOIR OF LIEUT. RUDOLPH DE LISLE, R.N., of the Naval Brigade. By the Rev. H. N. OXENHAM, M.A. Third Edition. With Illustrations. Crown 8vo. 7s. 6d.

EXPERIENCES OF A WOOLWICH PROFESSOR DURING FIFTEEN YEARS AT THE ROYAL MILITARY ACADEMY. By Major-General A. W. DRAYSON, late R.A., F.R.A.S., Author of "Practical Military Surveying," etc. Demy 8vo. 8s.

LORD BLOOMFIELD'S MISSION TO THE COURT OF BERNADOTTE. By GEORGIANA BARONESS BLOOMFIELD, Author of "Reminiscences of Court and Diplomatic Life." 2 vols. Demy 8vo. With Portraits. 28s.

THE FIRST NAPOLEON'S LETTERS AND DISPATCHES: A Selection from, with Explanatory Notes. By Captain the Hon. D. A. BINGHAM, Author of "Marriages of the Bonapartes." 3 vols. Demy 8vo. 42s.

LIFE AND CORRESPONDENCE OF RICHARD COBDEN. By JOHN MORLEY. Crown 8vo, with Portrait, 7s. 6d. Popular Edition, with Portrait, 4to, sewed, 1s.; bound in cloth, 2s.

GENERAL GORDON'S LETTERS FROM THE CRIMEA, THE DANUBE, AND ARMENIA. Second Edition. Crown 8vo. 5s.

FREDERICK THE GREAT. By Colonel C. B. BRACKENBURY. With Maps and Portrait. Large crown 8vo. 4s.

LOUDON : A Sketch of the Military Life of Gideon Ernest, Freicherr von Loudon, sometime Generalissimo of the Austrian Forces. By Colonel G. B. MALLESON, C.S.I. With Portrait and Maps. Large crown 8vo. 4s.

TURENNE. By H. M. HOZIER. With Portrait and Two Maps. Large crown 8vo. 4s.

PARLIAMENTARY GENERALS OF THE GREAT CIVIL WAR. By Major WALFORD, R.A. With Maps. Large crown 8vo. 4s.

THE LIFE OF CHARLES DICKENS. By JOHN FORSTER. With Illustrations. 2 vols. Demy 8vo, 20s. Post 8vo, 10s. 6d. 2 vols. 7s. Crown 4to, cloth, 5s.

WALTER SAVAGE LANDOR : a Biography, 1775–1864. By JOHN FORSTER. With Portrait. A New and Revised Edition. Demy 8vo. 12s.

FRIEDRICH FRÖBEL: a Short Sketch of his Life, including Fröbel's Letters from Dresden and Leipzig to his Wife, now first Translated into English. By EMILY SHIRREFF. Crown 8vo. 2s.

FRENCH REVOLUTIONARY GENERALS. By Major ARTHUR GRIFFITHS, H.M. Inspector of Prisons. Large crown 8vo. [*In the press.*

CREATORS OF THE AGE OF STEEL. Memoirs of Sir W. Siemens, Sir H. J. Bessemer, Sir J. Whitworth, Sir J. Brown, and other Inventors. By W. T. JEANS. Second Edition. Crown 8vo. 7s. 6d.

RAPHAEL : his Life, Works, and Times. By EUGENE MUNTZ. Illustrated with about 200 Engravings. A New Edition, revised from the Second French Edition. By W. ARMSTRONG, B.A. Imperial 8vo. 25s.

THE EARL OF PETERBOROUGH AND MONMOUTH (Charles Mordaunt): a Memoir. By Colonel FRANK RUSSELL, Royal Dragoons. With Illustrations. 2 vols. Demy 8vo. 32s.

A GIRL'S LIFE EIGHTY YEARS AGO. Selections from the Letters of ELIZA SOUTHGATE BOWNE. With an Introduction by CLARENCE COOK. Illustrated with Portraits and Views. Fcap. 4to. 12s.

RECOLLECTIONS OF FORTY YEARS. By FERDINAND DE LESSEPS. Translated from the French by C. B. PITMAN. 2 vols. Demy 8vo. 24s.

HISTORY, THEOLOGY, ART, ETC.

ART IN THE MODERN STATE. By Lady DILKE. Demy 8vo. 9s.

EVOLUTION OF ANCIENT HINDUISM. By A. M. FLOYER. Crown 8vo. 2s. 6d.

THE FIRST PRINCIPLES OF PHYSIOGRAPHY. By J. DOUGLAS. Crown 8vo. [*In December.*

THIRTY THOUSAND YEARS OF THE EARTH'S PAST HISTORY.
By Major-General A. W. DRAYSON, F.R.A.S., Author of "A Woolwich Professor," etc. Large crown 8vo. 5s.

THE PRINCIPLES OF AGRICULTURAL PRACTICE AS AN INSTRUCTIONAL SUBJECT. By J. WRIGHTSON, M.R.A.C., F.C.S., etc.; Professor of Agriculture in the Normal School of Science and Royal School of Mines. With Geological Map. Crown 8vo. 5s.

THE CHRONICLES OF BOW STREET POLICE OFFICE. With an Account of the Magistrates, "Runners," and Police; and a Selection of the most interesting Cases. By PERCY FITZGERALD, F.S.A. With numerous Illustrations. 2 vols. Demy 8vo. 21s.

AUSTRIAN HEALTH RESORTS AND THE BITTER WATERS OF HUNGARY. By W. FRASER RAE. Crown 8vo. 5s.

STUDIES NEW AND OLD. By W. L. COURTNEY, M.A., LL.D., of New College, Oxford. Crown 8vo. 6s.

CONSTRUCTIVE ETHICS: a Review of Modern Moral Philosophy in its Three Stages of Interpretation, Criticisms, and Reconstruction. By W. L. COURTNEY, M.A., LL.D. Demy 8vo. 12s.

A HISTORY OF VAGRANTS AND VAGRANCY AND BEGGARS AND BEGGING. By C. J. RIBTON-TURNER. Demy 8vo. 21s.

THE BASTILLE. By Capt. the Hon. D. BINGHAM, Author of "The Letters and Despatches of the First Napoleon." With Illustrations. 2 vols. Demy 8vo. 32s.

MODERN SCIENCE AND MODERN THOUGHT. By S. LAING. Sixth Edition. Demy 8vo. 3s. 6d.

CHAPTERS IN EUROPEAN HISTORY. With an Introductory Dialogue on the Philosophy of History. By W. S. LILLY. 2 vols. Demy 8vo. 21s.

ANCIENT RELIGION AND MODERN THOUGHT. By W. S. LILLY. Third Edition. Demy 8vo. 12s.

ENGLAND: ITS PEOPLE, POLITY, AND PURSUITS. By T. H. S. ESCOTT. A New and Revised Edition. Fifth Thousand. Demy 8vo. 8s.

EVOLUTION AND ITS RELATIONS TO RELIGIOUS THOUGHT. By J. LE CONTE, Professor of Geology and Natural History in the University of California. Crown 8vo. 6s.

DECORATIVE DESIGN. An Elementary Text-book of Principles and Practice. By FRANK G. JACKSON, Master, Birmingham Municipal School of Art. Fully Illustrated. Large crown 8vo, 7s. 6d.

THE FRENCH STAGE IN THE EIGHTEENTH CENTURY. By FREDERICK HAWKINS. With Portraits. 2 vols. Demy 8vo. 30s.

ANNALS OF THE FRENCH STAGE: FROM ITS ORIGIN TO THE DEATH OF RACINE. By FREDERICK HAWKINS. 4 Portraits. 2 vols. Demy 8vo. 28s.

THE BRITISH ARMY. By the Author of "The Present Position of European Politics." Demy 8vo. 12s.

THE PRESENT POSITION OF EUROPEAN POLITICS; or, Europe in 1887. By the Author of "Greater Britain." Demy 8vo. 12s.

HISTORY OF THE PEOPLE OF ISRAEL TILL THE TIME OF KING DAVID. By ERNEST RENAN. Translated from the French by C. B. PITMAN. Demy 8vo. 14s.

THE TSHI-SPEAKING PEOPLES OF THE GOLD COAST OF WEST AFRICA: their Religion, Manners, Customs, Laws, Language, etc. By A. B. ELLIS, Major, the 1st West Indian Regiment. With Map. Demy 8vo. 10s. 6d.

HISTORY OF ENGLAND. From the year 1830 to the Resignation of the Gladstone Ministry, 1874. By the Rev. W. NASSAU MOLESWORTH. Twelfth Thousand. 3 vols. Crown 8vo. 18s.

SKETCHES OF HINDOO LIFE. By DEVENDRA N. DÂS. Crown 8vo. 5s.

DAIRY FARMING. To which is added a Description of the Chief Continental Systems. With numerous Illustrations. By JAMES LONG. Crown 8vo. 9s.

PADDY AT HOME; or, IRELAND AND THE IRISH AT THE PRESENT TIME, AS SEEN BY A FRENCHMAN, BARON E. DE MANDAT-GRANCEY. Translated from the French. Fourth Edition. Crown 8vo. 2s.

JESUS CHRIST; GOD; AND GOD AND MAN. Conferences delivered at Notre Dame in Paris. PÈRE LACORDAIRE. New Edition. Crown 8vo. 6s.

COOKERY.

THE PYTCHLEY BOOK OF REFINED COOKERY AND BILLS OF FARE. By Major L——. Second Edition. Large crown 8vo. 8s.

BREAKFASTS, LUNCHEONS, AND BALL SUPPERS. By Major L——. Crown 8vo. 4s.

OFFICIAL HANDBOOK OF THE NATIONAL TRAINING SCHOOL FOR COOKERY. Containing Lessons on Cookery; forming the Course of Instruction in the School. Compiled by "R. O. C." Eighteenth Thousand. Large crown 8vo. 6s.

BREAKFAST AND SAVOURY DISHES. By "R. O. C." Seventh Thousand. Crown 8vo. 1s.

HOW TO COOK FISH. Compiled by "R. O. C." Crown 8vo, sewed. 3d.

SICK-ROOM COOKERY. Compiled by "R. O. C." Crown 8vo, sewed. 6d.

THE ROYAL CONFECTIONER; English and Foreign. A Practical Treatise. By C. E. FRANCATELLI. With numerous Illustrations. Fifth Thousand. Crown 8vo. 5s.

THE KINGSWOOD COOKERY BOOK. By H. F. WICKEN. Crown 8vo. 2s.

CHARLES DICKENS'S WORKS.

CHRISTMAS BOOKS.
MARTIN CHUZZLEWIT.
DAVID COPPERFIELD.
OLIVER TWIST.
GREAT EXPECTATIONS.
NICHOLAS NICKLEBY.
SKETCHES BY "BOZ."
CHRISTMAS STORIES.
THE PICKWICK PAPERS.
BARNABY RUDGE.
BLEAK HOUSE.
EDWIN DROOD: AND OTHER STORIES.

AMERICAN NOTES AND PICTURES FROM ITALY.
THE OLD CURIOSITY SHOP.
A CHILD'S HISTORY OF ENGLAND.
DOMBEY AND SON.
A TALE OF TWO CITIES.
LITTLE DORRIT.
MUTUAL FRIEND.
HARD TIMES.
UNCOMMERCIAL TRAVELLER.
REPRINTED PIECES.

THE CABINET EDITION.

In 32 vols. fcap. 8vo, Marble Paper sides, Cloth backs, with uncut edges, £2. 8s.
Each Volume contains Eight Illustrations reproduced from the Originals.

EIGHTEENPENCE EACH VOLUME.

THE ILLUSTRATED LIBRARY EDITION.

With all the Original Illustrations, in 30 vols. demy 8vo, £15; separate volumes, 10s. each.

THE HOUSEHOLD EDITION.

Complete, with Life by JOHN FORSTER. 22 vols. crown 4to, cloth, £4 8s. 6d.
Volumes sold separately.

THE "CHARLES DICKENS" EDITION.

With Illustrations.

Complete, with Life by JOHN FORSTER, and Letters. 25 vols. crown 8vo, £4 11s.
Volumes sold separately.

THE POPULAR LIBRARY EDITION.

Each volume containing 16 full-page Illustrations.
Complete in 30 vols. post 8vo, £6; separate volumes, 4s. each.

LIBRARY EDITION.

With the Original Illustrations.
Complete in 30 vols. post 8vo, cloth, £12; separate volumes, 8s. each.

THOMAS CARLYLE'S WORKS.

SARTOR RESARTUS.
FRENCH REVOLUTION.
LIFE OF JOHN STERLING.
OLIVER CROMWELL'S LETTERS AND SPEECHES.
ON HEROES AND HERO WORSHIP.
CRITICAL AND MISCELLANEOUS ESSAYS.
PAST AND PRESENT.
LATTER-DAY PAMPHLETS.
LIFE OF SCHILLER.
FREDERICK THE GREAT.
WILHELM MEISTER.
TRANSLATIONS FROM MUSÆUS, TIECK, AND RICHTER.
EARLY KINGS OF NORWAY, AND GENERAL INDEX.

ASHBURTON EDITION.
17 vols, demy 8vo, £6 16s.; separate volumes, 8s. each.

CHEAP AND UNIFORM EDITION.
In 23 vols. crown 8vo, £7 5s. Volumes sold separately.

LIBRARY EDITION.
34 vols, demy 8vo, £15. Volumes sold separately.

PEOPLE'S EDITION.
37 vols. small crown 8vo, cloth, £1 17s.; separate volumes, 1s. each.

ANTHONY TROLLOPE'S WORKS.

THE CHRONICLES OF BARSETSHIRE.
A Uniform Edition, in 8 vols. large crown 8vo, handsomely printed, each vol. containing Frontispiece. 6s. each.

THE WARDEN AND BARCHESTER TOWERS. 2 vols.
DR. THORNE.
FRAMLEY PARSONAGE.
THE SMALL HOUSE AT ALLINGTON. 2 vols.
LAST CHRONICLE OF BARSET. 2 vols.

GEORGE MEREDITH'S WORKS.

A New and Uniform Edition. In 10 vols., crown 8vo.

DIANA OF THE CROSSWAYS.
EVAN HARRINGTON.
THE ORDEAL OF RICHARD FEVEREL.
THE ADVENTURES OF HARRY RICHMOND.
SANDRA BELLONI. Originally EMILIA IN ENGLAND.
VITTORIA.
RHODA FLEMING.
BEAUCHAMP'S CAREER.
THE EGOIST.
THE SHAVING OF SHAGPAT: AN ARABIAN ENTERTAINMENT; AND FARINA.

CHAPMAN AND HALL, LIMITED, LONDON.

www.ingramcontent.com/pod-product-compliance
Lightning Source LLC
Chambersburg PA
CBHW031941230426
43672CB00010B/2005